VOLUME ONE HUNDRED AND TWO

ADVANCES IN
COMPUTERS

VOLUME ONE HUNDRED AND TWO

Advances in
COMPUTERS

Edited by

ALI R. HURSON
Missouri University of Science and Technology,
Rolla, MO, United States

MAZIAR GOUDARZI
Sharif University of Technology,
Tehran, Iran

AMSTERDAM • BOSTON • HEIDELBERG • LONDON
NEW YORK • OXFORD • PARIS • SAN DIEGO
SAN FRANCISCO • SINGAPORE • SYDNEY • TOKYO
Academic Press is an imprint of Elsevier

Academic Press is an imprint of Elsevier
50 Hampshire Street, 5th Floor, Cambridge, MA 02139, USA
525 B Street, Suite 1800, San Diego, CA 92101-4495, USA
The Boulevard, Langford Lane, Kidlington, Oxford OX5 1GB, UK
125 London Wall, London, EC2Y 5AS, UK

First edition 2016

Notices
Knowledge and best practice in this field are constantly changing. As new research and experience broaden our understanding, changes in research methods, professional practices, or medical treatment may become necessary.

Practitioners and researchers must always rely on their own experience and knowledge in evaluating and using any information, methods, compounds, or experiments described herein. In using such information or methods they should be mindful of their own safety and the safety of others, including parties for whom they have a professional responsibility.

To the fullest extent of the law, neither the Publisher nor the authors, contributors, or editors, assume any liability for any injury and/or damage to persons or property as a matter of products liability, negligence or otherwise, or from any use or operation of any methods, products, instructions, or ideas contained in the material herein.

ISBN: 978-0-12-809919-3
ISSN: 0065-2458

For information on all Academic Press publications
visit our website at https://www.elsevier.com/

  Working together
to grow libraries in
developing countries

www.elsevier.com • www.bookaid.org

Publisher: Zoe Kruze
Acquisition Editor: Zoe Kruze
Editorial Project Manager: Sarah Lay
Production Project Manager: Surya Narayanan Jayachandran
Cover Designer: Victoria Pearson

Typeset by SPi Global, India

CONTENTS

PREFACE

Traditionally, *Advances in Computers*, the oldest series to chronicle the rapid evolution of computing, annually publishes several volumes, each typically comprised of four to eight chapters, describing new developments in the theory and applications of computing. The theme of this 102nd volume is inspired by the advances in information technology. Within the spectrum of information technology this volume touches a variety of topics ranging from historical advances in software engineering, privacy challenges in mHealth systems, data cleansing techniques for cyber-physical systems, and indexing techniques for moving objects. The volume is a collection of four chapters that were solicited from authorities in the field, each of whom brings to bear a unique perspective on the topic.

In Chapter 1, "Advances in Software Engineering and Software Assurance," Shoemaker *et al.* survey the evolution of software engineering and software assurance from its inception to the present time. Technological advances in the areas of programming languages, personal computers, advances in intranet and Internet, and complex software applications are traced. The chapter also articulates the growth of cyber-attacks and vulnerability of information as the by-product of the aforementioned advances. Finally, this chapter skillfully ties together the advances that on the surface seem to be unrelated.

In Chapter 2, "Privacy Challenges and Goals in mHealth Systems," Rahman *et al.* address the scope and scale of mobile-based health (mHealth) systems emphasizing on the privacy issues. In an mHealth system, mobile devices, mainly sensors that may be attached to the patient's body, are used to capture and analyze the information gathered from patients and to communicate this information to health practitioners. Protection of medical information from unauthorized accesses and ensuring privacy of sensitive medical data bring out several challenges that are the main focus of this chapter.

In Chapter 3, "A Survey of Data Cleansing Techniques for Cyber-Physical Critical Infrastructure Systems," Woodard *et al.* articulate the dependence of critical cyber-physical systems on accurate data to facilitate intelligent control and improve performance. Corrupted data either intentionally or unintentionally have severe economical and safety consequences in a cyber-physical system. This chapter reviews techniques that are developed to detect and mitigate corrupted data. In addition, it addresses the applicability of these techniques to various control levels in a cyber-physical system.

Finally, in Chapter 4, "Indexing and Querying Techniques for Moving Objects in Both Euclidean Space and Road Network," Heendaliya *et al.* discuss research challenges due to the sheer size and volatility of data sources generated by moving objects either within a Euclidean space or road networks. Several data organizations that are intended to reduce the number of accesses and hence to allow fast retrieval are surveyed and comparatively analyzed against each other. The chapter also surveys several classes of queries for mobile objects. Finally, the chapter analyzes two classes of queries, namely snapshot and continuous queries, for mobile objects.

We hope that you find these articles of interest, and useful in your teaching, research, and other professional activities. We welcome feedback on the volume, and suggestions for future volumes.

A.R. HURSON

Missouri University of Science and Technology, Rolla, MO, United States

M. GOUDARZI

Sharif University of Technology, Tehran, Iran

CHAPTER ONE

Advances in Software Engineering and Software Assurance

D. Shoemaker*, C. Woody[†], N.R. Mead[†]

*Center for Cybersecurity, University of Detroit Mercy, Detroit, MI, United States
[†]CERT, Software Engineering Institute, Carnegie Mellon University, Pittsburgh, PA, United States

Contents

Advances in Computers, Volume 102
ISSN 0065-2458
http://dx.doi.org/10.1016/bs.adcom.2016.05.001

1

Abstract

In this chapter, the authors describe the evolution of software engineering (SE) and software assurance (SwA) from the days of punch cards until today. The authors create the backdrop for this development by describing the environment over the last 50 years. Technological advances during that period include the creation of programming languages, personal computers, the intranet, organized incident management, structured programming, and complex software applications. Impacts of these advances, including the massive growth of the Internet and software-intensive products, transformed everyday lives.

While these changes were happening, cyberattacks were also growing. Dating back to the late 1960s when phone systems were attacked, society has been affected by the "dark side" of computer technology. Computer viruses and malware are a common aspect of today's landscape. To protect us and our data, laws that govern the protection of computer data were created and developed. Likewise, organizations and approaches for finding and addressing cyberattacks were established and grown.

Education has supported this radically changing environment through the development of educational programs in industry and academia, including bachelor's and master's degree programs. SE education responded to the advancing technology, resulting in a new profession. SwA education responded to the failures of industry to develop quality software, including security challenges that arose as technology was used and exploited.

ABBREVIATIONS

ABET Adult Basic Education and Training
ACM Association for Computing Machinery
ADW Advanced Design Workshop
AL Assembly Language
ARPANET Algorithmic Language
BNF Backus–Naur Form
BOK body of knowledge
BSI Build Security In
CAPEC Common Attack Pattern Enumeration and Classification
CCCA Comprehensive Crime Control Act
CERT/CC CERT Coordination Center
CFAA Computer Fraud and Abuse Act
CMM Capability Maturity Model
CMU Carnegie Mellon University
CNSS Committee on National Security Systems
COTS commercial off-the-shelf
CSAB Computer Science Accreditation Board
CSDP Certified Software Development Professional
CSEE Conference on Software Engineering Education
CVE Common Vulnerabilities and Exposures
CWE Common Weakness Enumeration
DARPA Defense Advanced Research Projects Administration
DDOS distributed denial of service
DHS Department of Homeland Security
ETH Eidgenössische Technische Hochschule
EU European Union
FIPS Federal Information Processing Standards
FISMA Federal Information Security Management Act
ICT information and communications technology
IEEE Institute of Electrical and Electronics Engineers
IEEE-CS Institute of Electrical and Electronics Engineers Computer Society
IG inspector general
ISAP Information Security Automation Program
ISO/IEC International Organization for Standardization/International Electrotechnical Commission

MIT Massachusetts Institute of Technology
MS-DOS Microsoft Disk Operating System
MSE master's in software engineering
MVS Multiple Virtual Storage
NATO North Atlantic Treaty Organization
NDAA National Defense Appropriation Act
NIST National Institute of Standards and Technology
NSFNET National Science Foundation Network
NVD National Vulnerability Database
OEM original equipment manufacturer
OMB Office of Management and Budget
PC personal computer
RBN Russian Business Network
SAGE Strategic Advisors to Government Executives
SCAMP Special Computer APL Machine Portable
SCAP security content automation protocol
SCRM supply chain risk management
SDW Structured Design Workshop
SE software engineering
SEI Software Engineering Institute
SPW Structured Programming Workshop
SwA software assurance
SWEBOK Software Engineering Body of Knowledge
SWECC Software Engineering Coordinating Committee
TCP/IP Transmission Control Protocol/Internet Protocol
US-CERT United States Computer Emergency Readiness Team
WGSEET Working Group for Software Engineering Education and Training

1. INTRODUCTION

This chapter discusses significant software engineering (SE) advances that have occurred over the past 50 years in the light of the historical evolution of the technology. The thesis is that major advances in the way the profession goes about its business tends to appear in the form of specific responses to technological evolution.

In essence, we are saying that new requirements for large-scale processes and practices are typically shaped by significant new realties in the growth of the field of computing. Those practices will emerge as computer technology and its uses evolve. The implication of that statement is that the field of computing has developed its standard methods and practices in response to new challenges as they appear, rather than as a consequence of a series of planned, logical evolutionary stages.

That is not to say that the evolution of the practices in the field is illogical or that breakthroughs cannot be predicted. It is just to suggest that traditionally important aspects of the field are more likely to emerge and be institutionalized as advances in technology shine the spotlight on a new area of concern or need.

Both proactive and reactive solutions will emerge in detail from that recognition and seek to gain traction. Those solutions tend to be in the form of changes in the conduct of professional work, usually combined with some form of best SE practice. Once a given approach or practice gains the necessary traction, then it is used for leverage in tackling the next spotlight issue in a cascading evolutionary form.

Hence, this chapter will trace the evolution of the field, looking at a set of advances that might, on the surface, seem to be unrelated. However, it will be shown that they are all tied together by the natural proclivity of the industry to develop effective, real-world solutions to emerging challenges. Specifically, all of these changes center on the emergence of new technological advances and societal factors that have led to mass awareness. The shape and evolution of the resulting practice or process can be understood in the light of that pragmatic tendency.

This broad rule will be discussed from a larger historical perspective. The evidence is equivocal, to some extent, in its particulars. But the general pattern throughout the history of the profession is clearly apparent. Major influences in computing processes, practices, and education will evolve with the technology rather than lead it.

In presenting this idea, the orientation of this chapter will be practical and narrative, rather than theoretical. We will trace the historical course of events as they have occurred and discuss the commonly accepted principles, practices, and educational advances that emerged from significant developments in the overall field of computer technology.

The aim will be to demonstrate the general assumption that practices will emerge and grow as technology advances have required. Fig. 1 shows a timeline of the associated educational events [1].

Accordingly, the discussion itself will evolve and be driven by historical occurrences in the profession. For each occurrence, we will describe what happened in the context of the existing state of the art in the field. Then we will describe the response as it was developed and implemented. Finally, we will attempt to fit that response within the larger framework of our thesis, which is that the field evolves as the technology changes.

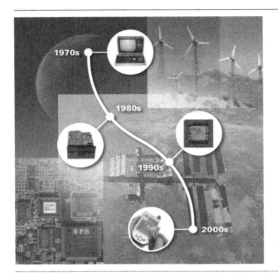

1968s
the term *software engineering* first appears
"go-to considered harmful" discussion published

1970s
IBM offers structured programming and design training
first MSE programs offered
first software engineering books published

1980s
Software Engineering Institute founded at Carnegie Mellon
first Conference on SE Education takes place
MSE model curriculum developed

1990s
Forum for the Advancement of SE Education starts
SEI CSEE becomes IEEE Computer Society CSEET
undergraduate SE degree programs accredited
industry–university collaborations grow
Texas Board votes to license software engineers
distance learning enables global SE education
IEEE-CS Software Engineering Code of Ethics established

2000s
IEEE-CS adopts SWEBOK
ASEET becomes part of CSEET
IEEE-CS offers CSDP certification program
many universities offer international SE programs
SE education tracks introduced in other conferences

Fig. 1 A timeline of software engineering education.

2. STRUCTURED PROGRAMMING: THE DAWN OF A NEW ERA

Structured programming might arguably be considered the first example of a major change in SE that came as a result of advances in the technology. In fact, strictly speaking, the term "structured programming" predates the term "software engineering."

The concept of structured programming was first introduced by Bohm and Jacopini in a paper published by the ACM in 1966 [2]. The term "software engineering" first appeared as the title of a conference sponsored by the North Atlantic Treaty Organization (NATO) Science Committee, which was held in Garmisch-Partenkirchen Germany in 1968 [3].

2.1 The GOTO Statement

The structured programming theorem, as first proposed by Bohn and Jacopini, was based around the utilization of three standard control structures: "sequence," "selection," and "iteration." In simple terms, the failure to properly document the jumps created by the GOTO statement led to overly complex and tangled code. This confusion had begun to negatively impact the understandability, maintainability, and effectiveness of commercial programs [4].

That problem led Edsger Djikstra to speculate that the GOTO statement in the procedural languages of the time led to poor programming practice. In essence, the overuse of jumps as a means of altering sequence had led many commercial programs into a "rat's nest" of unmaintainable applications and dead-end processing. Djikstra's initial idea was published as a letter in the Communications of the ACM in 1968 [4].

2.2 Structured Programming as a Solution

Djikstra's idea led to the evolution of the concept that the structured programming theorem was a solution to the "spaghetti code" problem. The control structures posited by the structured programming theorem allowed programmers to write and execute subroutines much more easily and effectively and create block programming constructions [2].

The goal of structured programming was to improve understanding of the code structure by normalizing the actual programming into standard subroutines. The contention was that structured programming would both improve quality and cut down on the cost of development by simplifying program execution into subroutines that execute within three types of control structures: sequence, selection, and iteration [2].

2.3 IBM Training

The advantages of structured programming were apparent to Harlan Mills of IBM. He convinced John Jackson, then president of IBM Federal Systems Division, to offer a series of courses titled "Structured Programming Workshop," "Structured Design Workshop," and eventually "Advanced Design Workshop," fondly known as SPW, SDW, and ADW [1].

SPW and SDW included exams that determined whether or not attendees passed the course. SPW emphasized not only structured programming but also formal correctness proofs. Every programmer in the division was to take SPW, which was a 2-week course preceded by a self-study and exam in logic. Lead programmers were to take SDW, which focused on the use of the state machine model to express abstractions, and the elite would eventually take ADW. ADW focused on issues of concurrency and timeliness, as represented by networks of state machines and associated operations. Eventually, these course offerings were supplemented by a

Table 1 IBM Software Engineering Course Curriculum

Courses	Audience
Logical Expression (prerequisite)	Programmers and software managers
Structured Programming Workshop	Programmers and software managers
Structured Design Workshop	Lead programmers and software managers
Advanced Design Workshop	Lead programmers doing concurrent design
Software Management Workshop	Software managers
University Courses	Electives

software management workshop (SMW) and university short courses. The curriculum is shown in Table 1.

While offering employee training on this scale now seems more commonplace, taking programmers off the job for 2–3 weeks and housing them at a central location was a big commitment at the time. The division had around 10–12 thousand staff members then, of which some 2500 or so were programmers.

However, given that people in the industry did not change jobs very often, there was an opportunity for the company to reap the benefits of having better educated and trained practitioners. Workshop completions were tracked at the highest levels of management. The workshops resulted in the Linger–Mills–Witt book on structured programming [5], which is still in use.

3. LANGUAGE SUPPORT FOR STRUCTURED PROGRAMMING

The structured programming control structures required two significant evolutionary changes in the technology to become relevant and possible.

3.1 FORTRAN

The first of these was the advent of compiler-based languages (1957) [6]. In the mid-1950s, IBM's John Backus headed a team that defined the first high-level general purpose imperative language [6]. It was called FORTRAN (Formula Translator) and it was first operational in April of 1957 [6].

FORTRAN was proposed as an alternative to assembly language (AL), which was the only programming utility available at the time. AL had been specifically designed to make the IBM 704 easier to use [6].

Early programming was mostly limited to punched card input, and FORTRAN's structure accommodated that by assigning fixed columns to certain required computer functions. Columns 1–5 were designated as operators [6]. Besides enabling a FORMAT, READ, or WRITE ability, those columns allowed a GOTO capability. GOTO was useful for jump purposes, should the programmer need to alter the execution sequence of a Von Neumann architecture machine [6]. GOTO allowed for much more flexible and complex applications.

3.2 ALGOL 60

FORTRAN was followed by other compiler languages in the late 1950s, such as CODASYL's COBOL (1959). But it was a refinement of compiler technology through the advent of ALGOL 60 that made the structured programming theorem practical. This new compiler language underwrote the ability to develop structured code. ALGOL 60 is of considerable interest in a discussion of structured programming because it provided the facility for implementing the control structures suggested by the structured programming theorem.

Specifically, it featured three key innovative language functions: code blocks and entry/exit delimiters, nested functions creating the capability for information hiding, and notational design languages [7]. The proposal for notational design languages was carried into ALGOL by John Backus, the father of FORTRAN.

The approach he proposed permitted the concrete description of programming syntax. He introduced the concept of notation for representation of complex programming design for control structure functioning at the initial conference for the design of the ALGOL compiler at Eidgenössische Technische Hochschule (ETH) Zürich in 1958 [4]. This notation was documented in the 1960 report on ALGOL as Backus–Naur Form (BNF) [8].

BNF notation provided a context-free grammar for describing the "block structure" of the structured programming theorem [9]. Thus it is the root of the tree that has led to languages such as Pascal, C, C++, and Java. ALGOL was also the first language to implement BNF [10]. It also provided the facility for recursive calling of functions, which made block programming much more practical to implement [9].

3.3 Intersection of Languages and a New Paradigm

Because "spaghetti code" is so undesirable, it is likely that structured programming would have been adopted in some form and at some stage in the evolution of the profession. Nevertheless, it was the intersection of procedural language compilers and, specifically, the programming paradigm of the ALGOL language that allowed the practical implementation of the structured programming theorem's control structures and ensured that the structured programming approach could be implemented at that particular point in the history of the profession.

3.4 Software Engineering

Since the use of the paradigm elements of a procedural language like ALGOL is a higher level design issue, it also made perfect sense that the follow-on thinking to structured programming approach would turn to the issue of construction, specifically the discipline of SE. So it does not seem the least bit strange that the list of participants at the 1960 conference on ALGOL would contain some of the same names as the participants at the 1968 conference on SE: Naur and Bauer were two of these.

This is not to suggest that the ALGOL language shaped the discipline of SE; the LISP people [11], among others, would be able to dispute that. What it DOES suggest is that the thinking at the time regarding the need for a rational process of construction, from design down to code, was enabled by the presence of a real-world vehicle: the ALGOL language.

Moreover, because that practical vehicle was available, it was possible to offer a concrete solution to the ills of ad hoc programming. Finally, given the concepts of structure at the code level that ALGOL's programming paradigms allowed, the logical next step would be to encapsulate the same kind of structure into the development of software grounded in the application of the rigorous practices of engineering [8].

In effect, the development of third-generation procedural compilers and the language concepts of ALGOL provided the fertile ground for the growth of the discipline of SE. Would SE have appeared as a discipline without third-generation technologies? The answer to that question is "probably," since the techniques of SE have always been the most effective path to commercial programming in the large. Still, history demonstrates that whatever might have occurred was made possible at the actual point in time where compiler languages met a specific programming paradigm: structured programming.

One of the follow-on developments to structured programming and the associated mathematical proofs of correctness was the Cleanroom SE process [12] with its focus on defect prevention via rigorous software development methods. Much of the Cleanroom research and prototype work were led by Rick Linger at IBM Federal Systems in collaboration with Harlan Mills. In addition to rigorous mathematical proofs and formal inspections, statistical testing was one of the methods used to develop zero-defect software.

3.5 SE Education

As the SE discipline reached new levels, so did the education required for its effective practice. In the late 1970s, master's degree programs in SE began to emerge [1]. One of the very early programs was started at Wang Institute of Graduate Studies. Other early programs appeared at Seattle University and Texas Christian University.

The workshop series that was so successful in IBM's Federal Systems Division grew into a corporate-level commitment, and IBM's Software Engineering Institute (SEI) was founded in New York City. (It was later moved to Westchester County.) The corporate model was slightly different, but many of the same courses were offered across the company, and at the corporate level, in-house instructors were certified to teach them via a formal instructor training program. Dick Fairley wrote one of the first books on SE concepts [13] and went on to become a leader in SE education.

4. COMPUTING MEETS REALITY: THE PROTECTION OF INFORMATION IN COMPUTERS

The concept of transmitting data over networks predates the Internet by 150 years. Americans had been using Samuel Morse's little system long before the Civil War. And it was in that War that some of the techniques used by modern-day hackers, such as "man-in-the-middle," first appeared. Nonetheless, the concepts that underlie the networked transmission of computer data were consolidated and popularized in a paper by Licklider [14].

4.1 The SAGE and SABRE Networks

What we would eventually come to call commercial "networks" emerged in the early 1960s. There were military networks slightly earlier, primarily the SAGE network [15]. The SAGE network actually led to a fortuitous conversation, held between a high-ranking American Airlines executive and

Thomas J. Watson, who was the President of IBM. They happened to be sitting next to each other on the same airline flight.

In that conversation, it was mentioned that American was developing its own reservation system, and it became clear that the SAGE system was perfectly suited to American Airlines' booking needs [16]. That discussion in 1957 led to the joint American/IBM Semi-Automated Business Research Environment, or SABRE network, which was first fully operational on two IBM 7090 mainframes in 1960.

American Airlines' SABRE was the first practical everyday network operating in the United States. It handled 83,000 requests per day and far exceeded the capabilities of the manual systems used by the other airlines. At its inception, SABRE was a classic hardwired, physical network, dependent on copper wire to transmit its information.

4.2 ARPANET

About the same time that SABRE was coming into use, the Defense Advanced Research Projects Administration (DARPA) began a project to interconnect its main computers around the United States (Cheyenne Mountain, SAC Headquarters, and the Pentagon). Licklider was the leader of that effort [17]. Their product was rolled out in 1968 as the Advanced Research Projects Administration Network (ARPANET). Numerous luminaries in the existing field were involved in the initial development, but Paul Baran's packet-switching concepts were at the heart of the construction of ARPANET [18].

Initially, ARPANET and other seminal packet-switching networks had a very minimal footprint in common use. ARPANET first involved just two nodes (in October 1969) and then four nodes (in December 1969) [18]. Nevertheless, the genie was out of the bottle and expansion into the commercial world was achieved by the early 1970s. All that were required to get the foundation completed for the Internet was the creation of TCP/IP in 1975 [19].

4.3 Crime and Computers

While the technology base was being developed, the 1960s also saw a developing revolutionary culture. One of the subsets of that culture, the Yippies, published a newsletter in the late 1960s that was mainly oriented toward phone phreaking, but which had a definite hacker overtone. Meanwhile, the arrest of John Draper, better known as Captain Crunch, brought mainstream notoriety to the concept of criminality in the world of electronic communication.

While it was not extensively documented, it was clear that by the beginning of the 1970s that the ubiquity of networked technology had raised enough concerns about security to justify a response. Jerome Saltzer and Michael Schroeder make that clear in their discussion of the need for authority structures when there is simultaneous use of applications by several individuals [20].

Saltzer and Schroeder go on to cite the specific example of SABRE as one of the potential targets for attack, and they first popularize the issues of confidentiality, integrity, and availability of information, which continue to be of increasing concern across the public and private sectors.

4.4 Strategies for Protecting Data

Their pivotal paper was first presented at the Fourth ACM Symposium on Operating System Principles (October 1973) and then revised and published in the Publications of the ACM [20]. They proposed eight principles for the protection of information in computers. These eight principles have formed much of the basis for computer access control and overall mediation of computer security issues. Much of the literature of computer security starts from those fundamental principles [21].

The principles of Saltzer and Schroeder indeed proved significant, and what most interests us here is their TIMING. When their paper was first presented (1973), it was already acknowledged that the information that was processed by computers was valuable and had to be protected [20]. At the same time, the technology had advanced to the point where internetworked machines were no longer a scientific experiment conducted at ivy tower places like MIT and Stanford. They had become an integral part of the industry and national security.

4.5 Technology and Threats Converge

By 1972, IBM had fully commercialized its airline reservation systems. In addition, public data networks based on the X.25 standard prevailed throughout the large business networks in Europe and the United States. What had not matured, however, was the protection of the information in those networks.

There are no reliable statistics regarding incidents in that period, and law enforcement was focused more on phreaking than hacking. But the appearance of an Esquire article in 1971 (Ron Rosenbaum's Esquire article, "Secrets of the Little Blue Box") directed the spotlight onto the potential for attacks on internetworked machines [22].

Given this emerging level of threat, the professional community would be expected to begin to address information protection issues in networks. It might not be quite as probable to assume that the first well-known product would be as influential and enduring as Salter and Schroeder's work. Nevertheless, given the point to where the technology had matured, the challenges of computer security were of increasing urgency, and Saltzer and Schroeder addressed that concern with their principles.

For their information security to take priority, networks had to exist and become a growing phenomenon both in the government and in the business. That limited the time for reaching the growth threshold to the period around 1970, from a technological evolution standpoint. But there also had to be a recognition and impetus for formalizing security practice.

The popular media's obsession with phone phreaking provided the spark. Phreaking was a hot news item at the time because it was tied to the counterculture movement that was in full swing by 1971. Phreaking is relevant, even though the network that it focused on had been around since Alexander Graham Bell invented it. Nonetheless, given the vulnerability of networks at the time and the somewhat anarchistic zeitgeist of the early 1970s, a work like Salter and Schroeder's was begging to be published.

Considering these developments from the perspective of 2015 and how three essentially unrelated things were evolving and interrelating—network hardware technologies, data transmission protocols, and commercial business applications of computers—it seems inevitable that a security manifesto would be needed.

4.6 Before the Internet

However, at the time, the communities that were coming together to formulate the eventual product—the Internet—were only working toward their separate goals. While one technology factor, the development of distributed networks, suggests the need for the other requirement—a common, interoperable method of transmitting data—the combination of those two into a powerful force was still well in the future.

Time has shown the value and utility of the principles presented by Saltzer and Schroeder; however, it is appropriate to consider that these principles were developed prior to the Morris Worm, which generated a massive denial of service by infecting over 6000 UNIX machines on November 2,

1988. To provide a technology context, consider that the IBM System 360 was in use from 1964 to 1978 and the IBM System 370 came on the market in 1972. An advanced operating system MVS (multiple virtual storage) was released in March 1974.

Saltzer and Schroeder published their material prior to the identification of the over 66,900 software vulnerabilities and exposures that are currently exploitable in today's software products, as described in the common vulnerabilities and exposures (CVE) database at http://cve.mitre.org/.

When these principles were developed, "buffer overflow," "malicious code," "cross-site scripting," and "zero-day vulnerabilities" were not part of the everyday vocabulary of operational software support personnel. Patches were carefully tested and scheduled to minimize operational disruption instead of pushed into operation to minimize attack vectors.

While these principles are still usable today in regards to security within an individual piece of technology, they are no longer sufficient to address the complexity and sophistication of the environment within which that component must operate. We must broaden our horizon to consider the large scale, highly networked, software-dependent systems upon which all of our critical infrastructure depend—from phones to power and water and industries such as banking, medicine, and retail.

4.7 Software Assurance

"Software assurance" (SwA) is the term that has come into common usage to describe this broader context. The Committee on National Security Systems (CNSS) defines SwA as follows:

> *Software assurance (SwA) is the level of confidence that software is free from vulnerabilities, either intentionally designed into the software or accidentally inserted at any time during its life cycle, and that the software functions in the intended manner. [23]*

Vast lists of practices and procedures that describe what should be done to address security and SwA have been published. By the end of 2014, National Institute of Standards and Technology (NIST) had released over 114 guideline documents addressing various aspects of security and SwA controls.

Organizations are overwhelmed with the volume of controls and the implementation costs of security, and have often failed to consider the organizational impact of a successful attack. Motivation to address SwA requires, at a minimum, an understanding of what to do, how to go about it, and why it is needed.

Table 2 Software Assurance Principles

Principle Title	Brief Description
Perception of risk	Risk drives assurance decisions
Interactions	Risk is aligned across all stakeholders and all interconnected technology elements
Trusted dependencies	Dependencies are trusted
Attacker	There are no perfect protections against attacks
Coordination and education	Assurance is effectively coordinated among all technology participants
Well-planned and dynamic balance	Assurance is well-planned and dynamic
Measurability	A means to measure and audit overall assurance is built in

In response, the SEI released a set of seven SwA principles [24] that help an organization define what is needed and determine where to invest its security funds. These are shown in Table 2, with more detailed descriptions in the referenced paper.

5. SECURITY GETS SERIOUS: SOCIETAL RESPONSES AND THE MORRIS WORM

Internetworking technology continued to mature throughout the 1970s and 1980s. However, as we have seen, when technology evolves, history has shown that security issues will arise. With the convergence of internetworking capabilities comes the opportunity for attacks, or more specifically, the ability to perform remote, often distributed, malicious acts via a network. The initial attacks were by means of a virus.

5.1 Computer Viruses

A virus is simply a piece of malicious code inserted into a computer to perform undesirable acts. The first attributed virus was called *Creeper* and it was written by Robert Thomas as an experimental exercise in 1971 [25]. In the intervening 17 years, more than 15 attributed viruses appeared [25]. Among them were such influential exploits as Wabbit (1974), ANIMAL (1975), Elk Cloner (1982), Brain Boot (1986), Lehigh (1987), Jerusalem (1987), and Christmas Tree (1987) [25].

In the popular media, the term "Worm" (1975) actually preceded the term "virus" (1983) [25,26]. The description of a program that propagates itself first appeared in the science fiction novel "Shockwave Rider" [26]. The author, John Brunner, coined the term as an homage to J.R.R. Tolkien's "Great Worm."

It was in 1984 that Frederick Cohen coined the term "virus" [27]. His term was meant to describe any type of alien program that replicates itself in the same manner that a "virus" infection would take place. The "virus" could install itself in, or "infect," other programs [24]. By Cohen's definition, a software "virus" can "contaminate" other programs by inserting copies of itself into them, similar to the way a virus propagates [27].

5.2 Viruses "In the Wild"

So we see that the Morris Worm was not the first malicious exploit. Nonetheless, it differentiated itself from the other examples because it successfully operated on a networked system "in the wild."

A virus is considered to be "in the wild" if it propagates uncontained in the realm of the general user community due to normal operation. "A virus being studied in a controlled environment for research purposes would not be considered 'in the wild.' Also, a virus (or Trojan) that exists but is not actively spreading is not considered to be 'in the wild'" [28].

5.3 The Morris Worm

The Morris Worm is NOT the first virus to live outside of a research facility. That distinction goes to the Elk Cloner virus, which was written 5 years earlier with the intention of exploiting an Apple II vulnerability [27] and was only propagated by floppy disk [28]. Nor is the Morris Worm the first personal computer (PC) virus. Brain Boot, which was written a year earlier as a deterrent to software piracy, carries that distinction [28]. What the Morris Worm DID accomplish was to popularize the fact that the use of computers could be affected by uncontrollable external forces.

The Morris Worm was released into networks that contained elements that would eventually come to be called the "Internet." That release took place on November 2, 1988. The subsequent actions of the Worm shut down internetworked components of SFSNet and only affected VAX's running UNIX [29]. The resultant fork-type attack led to a partitioning of SFSNET, as the component networks began to disconnect to preserve their own service capability [29]. In addition to a 3-day denial of service, the fragmentation of the existing network was perhaps the most disturbing aspect [29].

5.4 The Computer Fraud and Abuse Act

The exploit is considered a landmark because it produced the first conviction under PL 99-474, "The Computer Fraud and Abuse Act," which had been passed 2 years earlier (1986). Morris was prosecuted mainly because of the extent of the damage. Public–Law 99-474, the Computer Fraud and Abuse Act (CFAA, 1986), is the first real law that addressed crimes committed using a computer. The CFAA was enacted by Congress in 1986. It amended the Comprehensive Crime Control Act of 1984 (CCCA, 18 U.S.C. Section 1030) [30].

It was probably inevitable at that point in the development of the proto-Internet that a law of this type would be written. TCP/IP had become the standard for internetworking by 1982 [31], and with the implementation of NSFNET in 1985, all the pieces were in place to do the sort of broad-scale communication that we see today on the commercial Internet [32]. In that respect, some form of regulation was required because the technology had approached the point where serious measures had to be taken to ensure that its users and the emerging infrastructure were protected from attack.

The CFAA was written to clarify and increase the scope of the previous version of the CCCA. The general aim was to legally apply federal sovereignty to cases "with a compelling federal interest, essentially electronic transmissions that cross state lines" [30]. In addition to clarifying a number of the provisions in the original section 1030, the CFAA also criminalized additional computer-related acts. Provisions addressed the distribution of malicious code and denial of service attacks. Congress also included a provision in the CFAA criminalizing trafficking in passwords and similar items [30].

The governance of interstate commerce is one of the exclusive powers given to the federal government in the U.S. constitution, so the authority for this action goes way back in time. The point for our discussion is that 1984 marks the point where wide-area network technologies were beginning to get serious traction in society at large and, more importantly, across state lines.

This act establishes through federal mandate that a person is in criminal violation of the law who

- knowingly accesses a computer without proper authorization;
- exceeds his/her permitted access;
- uses that access to cause a loss greater than $1000; and
- performs an act, such as launching a denial of service attack, that prevents other authorized users from using their computers.

The CFAA further prohibits unauthorized or fraudulent access to government computers. It specifically prohibits access with intent to defraud, and it prohibits intentional trespassing, which is the legal term for "hacking." The act is restricted to "federal interest computers," which is not as narrow as it might seem [30].

The act applies not only to computers that are owned by the government or used by the government. It specifically applies to computers used by federally insured financial institutions. It also applies to computers that access federal data or computers that are located in two or more states (eg, the Internet) [30], which extends federal jurisdiction into every nook and cranny of the private sector. The act makes it a misdemeanor to post stolen passwords or obtain or even look at the data in a computer that fits that provision, such as bank data [30]. The law makes it a felony to alter or destroy information in a computer that falls under that designation, if the loss is over $1000 [30].

5.5 Punishment Under the Law

In the 10 years before the advent of the commercial Internet, the CFAA was intended to apply strictly to computers containing national defense, banking, or financial information. It established criteria for what would be considered criminal acts that took place in the computers to which the Act applied, ranging from a fine of $5000 or twice the value of the thing obtained by the illegal activity up to 5 years in jail for "criminal" offenses [30].

Robert T. Morris was convicted and sentenced under this law for the first true cybercrime (1989). As a point of interest, his case serves as a very good illustration of the problem of trying to assign penalties for crimes involving abstract actions like denials of service. Although his act was considered a "six" under normal sentencing guidelines such that he was found guilty of major felony fraud and deceit, the sentencing judge departed from the stipulations of the law and gave him 3 years of probation, a $10,000 fine, and 400 h of community service.

The Supreme Court upheld his conviction a year later by deciding not to hear his case. It was their opinion that the wording of PL 99-474 was sufficient to define the facts of unauthorized access. Their view was that the defendant had demonstrated sufficient intent to injure to justify his conviction under the Computer Fraud and Abuse Law's "authorization to access" provisions.

However, as it was worded, the PL 99-474 left no distinction between people who use computers for recreational hacking vs those who use it for crime or terrorism. A correction was made by the rather awkwardly titled

"Uniting and Strengthening America by Providing Appropriate Tools Required to Intercept and Obstruct Terrorism Act," or PATRIOT Act (2002). The Patriot Act changed a lot of the basic jurisprudence for cyber, but it is generally acknowledged to be the outcome of geopolitical events and therefore not relevant to our particular discussion.

What IS relevant is the fact that the Morris Worm is the first example of a distributed denial of service (DDOS) attack. Although the people using the Internet were a relatively limited group of academics and governmental types, in 1988 the potential for a massive shutdown of the existing networks led to widespread media coverage.

5.6 The CERT/CC

The issues raised by the news coverage were a significant factor in the creation of the CERT Coordination Center (CERT/CC), which included the original computer emergency response team (CERT) for Internet security incidents. In keeping with the general trend for the profession to respond as technological developments step into the media spotlight, the CERT/CC was developed at Carnegie Mellon University (CMU) in 1988 [33].

The CERT/CC was designated to address Internet threats so that the IT community could coordinate a response [33]. The CERT/CC was tasked in its mission statement to focus on improving both the practices and understanding of security and survivability issues relating to critical information infrastructures.

Its goal is to ensure that system developers and operators use appropriate technology and systems management practices to recognize, resist, and recover from attacks on networked systems [33]. The CERT Program partners with government, industry, law enforcement, and academia to develop advanced methods and technologies to counter large scale, sophisticated cyber threats [33].

The program draws heavily on the security incident and vulnerability data gained from its CERT/CC to further applied research and development efforts [33]. The SEI at CMU has operated the CERT/CC since 1988, providing a central response and coordination facility for global information security incident response and countermeasures for threats and vulnerabilities [33].

There have been other responses to the problems of Internet security, both legal and practical. Nevertheless, the CERT Division of the SEI was the first such response in the United States and its mission statement makes clear the source of its foundation. Without the technological advances embodied in the proto-Internet, there would be no need for the CERT Division's mission.

In addition, without the popular exposure that the Morris Worm brought to the problem of keeping internetworked communications free of harmful entities, there would probably have not been the political influences to underwrite that founding. This is not to suggest that an entity with the CERT Division's general mission and profile would not have existed without the Morris Worm. But the time was right from a technological standpoint and all that was required was the spark. Morris provided that.

6. SOFTWARE AS A COMMODITY AND THE RISE OF THE SE BEST PRACTICE APPROACH

Throughout the 1980s, software and systems became products sold commercially for general use rather than exercises in specialized development. The term for software or a system that is purchased as a commodity, not developed internally, is *commercial off-the-shelf* (COTS). COTS products can provide a number of important advantages, since only one organization must invest the development time and the costs of development are shared by all purchasers.

6.1 Personal Computers

The advent of software as a commodity can be traced to yet another massive change in the technology—the PC. Up to the late 1970s, computing was primarily a mainframe exercise. Large central processors and a network of dumb terminals and other peripherals were the state-of-the-art. The PC put into the hands of every person what had been, to that point, a rather arcane technology.

Mainframe machines required a high degree of system management knowledge and the software running on them was as massive as the computers they serviced. In addition, the software itself was often highly specialized for the mainframe operating systems it served and the cost of software was prohibitive to the normal buyer.

Small, easy-to-operate personal machines and their attendant operating systems and application software opened up a mass market for every conceivable consumer application from word processing to video games.

The earliest version of a PC, which at the time was called a "microcomputer," appeared in 1973 in the form of IBM's SCAMP [34]. SCAMP led directly to the IBM 51xx series in 1975 [34], which led to the IBM 5150 in 1981. The 5150 was the first open architecture version and can be considered the progenitor of today's ubiquitous PC.

The open architecture concept encouraged original equipment manufacturers (OEMs) to produce peripherals and even software to run on the 5150. This peripheral and software flexibility gave IBM most of the market share that Apple had not already grabbed with the Apple II.

6.2 Application Software

Thus, along with OEM peripheral manufacture, the various forms of application software to run on such computers became very big business indeed. Ten years after the initial launch of a very rudimentary MS-DOS-based PC, IBM MS-DOS-based applications composed 65% of the computer-game market, with the Commodore Amiga at 10%; all other computers, including the Apple Macintosh, were below 10% and declining [35].

The profits from the huge increase in the sales of software as a product grew steadily larger as the decade of the 1980s rolled along. A robust market for commercial software led to an ever increasing inventory of COTS products. Time to market became an increasing concern, as a competitor could quickly render a product obsolete, reducing the seller's ability to recapture investment. Of course, the downside to all of the availability was the issue of the quality of the products.

The tendency toward lower cost "buy" not "make" decisions created the commercial software market that we know today. Of course, the resultant commercialization of the code meant that the customer was completely dependent on the vendor for assurance of the quality and security of the product. Unfortunately, the vendor did not have the same assurance concerns as the buyer, which proved to be a source of a number of problems by the early 1990s.

Mainly, commercial software could not be trusted to function as planned. Currently, the commercial software business is a significant and hugely profitable industry. According to Gartner, a leading industry research organization, its annual global revenue was over $400 billion in 2013 [36]. Nonetheless, most information and communications technology (ICT) projects exceed their schedules or budgets in a way that would never be tolerated by customers in any other industry.

6.3 Flawed Software Development

For instance, a series of surveys conducted by the Standish Group found that 32% of all projects are delivered on time, on budget, with required features and functions, 44% were late, over budget, and/or delivered with less than the required features and functions, and 24% were cancelled prior to completion or delivered and never used [37]. Capers Jones has consistently found that, depending on project size, between 25% and 50% of all projects fail, where "failure" means that the project is canceled or grossly exceeds its schedule estimates [38].

A study done during the time period, we are considering found that fully two-thirds of the software delivered to the federal government was never used and an additional 29% was never delivered at all. The good news was that 3% was usable after changes and 2% could be used as delivered. As a result, it was estimated that throughout the decade of the 1980s the federal government's bill for worthless software topped $150 billion [39].

6.4 The Software Engineering Institute

When 95% of the software delivered to an entity like the federal government is worthless, you might expect some sort of response. During the early 1980s, a study was undertaken that resulted in establishment of the current SEI at CMU in 1984 [40]. The SEI's primary mission was to popularize and improve the practice of SE, which seeks to apply best practice engineering principles to the design, development, and maintenance of software.

In addition to improving SE practice, one of the key elements of the original SEI charter was to advance SE education [1]. Under the leadership of Norm Gibbs, SEI's Director of Education, the first Conference on Software Engineering Education (CSEE) took place in 1986/87. Many of our current leaders in SE were involved in these early activities, both inside and outside the SEI.

SE had been around as a theoretical construct since the 1968 conference that first defined its elements [3] and had been applied as a discipline to complex software projects, mainly at places like the IBM Federal Systems Division [41]. Nevertheless, the actual formal application of its principles in common everyday use can be traced directly to the founding of the SEI in 1984.

6.5 Master's in Software Engineering

As a consequence of the early education workshops and work at the SEI, the initial master's in software engineering (MSE) model curriculum was developed, and an MSE program was started at CMU in 1990 that continues to this day. Needless to say, the program has undergone changes in content and faculty since those early offerings.

The CMU MSE graduated its first class in 1991. The number of MSE programs grew rapidly, and during these years the SEI developed and distributed instructional materials in the form of videotaped courses, curriculum modules, and educational materials. Many universities used these early materials as a springboard, whereas others developed programs that were uniquely their own. Over time, the various programs came to reflect the specialties and emphasis of their universities [42].

6.6 Software Process

The SEI's mission at the time was to popularize the practices associated with the discipline of SE. That included the publication of Watts Humphrey's seminal work, "Characterizing the Software Process: A Maturity Framework," in June of 1987 and the subsequent Addison and Wesley text, "Managing the Software Process" [43,44].

The Capability Maturity Framework laid out in those two works would be revised into the Capability Maturity Model (CMM v1.1), which would essentially guide software practice throughout the next 20 years and shape the world's view of how to implement good practice in development, sustainment, and acquisition of software. The CMM as a set of defined best practices was published in 1995 [45].

Nevertheless, this breakthrough could not have happened until the technological and social factors that motivated it had progressed to the point where commonly accepted best practice needed to be brought into the mainstream. It was not that SE was not practiced as a discipline. But most SE was done in advanced settings like the space program. It took technological breakthroughs like PCs and business phenomena like the commercial software industry to make SE a major force in the world and the promoter of code quality and security.

6.7 WGSEET

In 1995, a working group for software engineering education and training (WGSEET) was formed. This was an ad hoc group whose goal was to advance SE education and training. The WGSEET provided a forum for advancing the field and for tackling controversial issues in a friendly environment. It continued for a number of years as a standalone group, publishing many useful papers and reports. Its topics included curriculum development, industry–university collaboration, and professionalism.

The WGSEET provided an opportunity to support SE curriculum development and publication. In fact, the work of the WGSEET preceded

SE curriculum development efforts by the professional societies, led by professionals such as Rich LeBlanc and Gerry Engel.

6.8 Undergraduate Software Development Degrees

About the same time, undergraduate degree programs in SE education started to emerge, and in the United States a merger of the accrediting bodies, CSAB and ABET, made it possible for them to be accredited. New curricula were developed to support a variety of computing degree programs [46]. Universities such as Rochester Institute of Technology, under the leadership of Mike Lutz, were pioneers in offering the first undergraduate degrees in SE in the United States [47].

Other countries, such as Australia, found it easier to offer undergraduate degrees in SE. Their accreditation processes examined engineering programs as a whole, and so they did not have to wrestle as much with the question of whether SE was a legitimate engineering discipline. In the EU, many of the SE offerings were in departments that taught computing, so once again the term "engineering" was not problematic for these universities.

It became clear that part of the SE education agenda was to collaborate with industry as well as influence it. The early MSE programs were among the roots of work in industry–university collaboration. Many universities established industry advisory boards so that their degree programs could remain relevant to their industry partners. These collaborations took many forms, such as joint research and regular work sessions or meetings.

6.9 SE as a Profession

To advance the profession, a joint committee was formed by ACM and IEEE Computer Society (IEEE-CS) in 1993 to promote SE as a profession. Dennis Frailey was cochair of the initial IEEE/ACM Steering Committee to Establish Software Engineering as a Profession (1994–1998) (and then vice-chair of the Software Engineering Coordinating Committee [SWECC] from 1999 to 2001). The SWECC supported the initial development of the Software Engineering Body of Knowledge (SWEBOK) [48].

The initial SWEBOK was a multiyear effort, with Robert Dupuis and Pierre Bourque serving as primary editors. There was an extensive process of multiple reviews and an industrial advisory board. Many professionals contributed to the effort. Once the SWEBOK was completed, some professionals saw it as the basis for certification programs, but others feared that it would become the basis for licensing. The SWEBOK has gone through a recent update cycle, and licensing of software engineers is less controversial, but still not widespread.

In that same timeframe, Don Gotterbarn led an effort to establish the Software Engineering Code of Ethics and Professional Practice [49] and an associated curriculum. His dedication to this effort in the face of controversy and his perseverance are noteworthy.

Licensing generated serious controversy among thoughtful people that continues to this day. Papers about licensing generated a level of rhetoric that had not been seen before [50,51]. More scholarly articles received fewer slings and arrows, but were nevertheless controversial [52]. Licensing has not become extensive in the United States, but it successfully faced legal challenges in Canada. More recently, licensing exams for professional software engineers have been developed.

IEEE-CS started to offer a certification program that was initially based on the SWEBOK and has evolved to include several levels of certification [53]. The exams were professionally developed and tested extensively. This program has been less controversial than licensing. The term "Certified Software Development Professional (CSDP)" avoids the use of the term "engineer."

7. THE RISE OF THE INTERNET AND THE ADVENT OF FORMAL SOFTWARE AND SYSTEM SECURITY PROGRAMS

7.1 The Early Internet

Since each technology use has also provided opportunities for abuse, it is no surprise that the technological advance that will probably go down in history as the watershed event of the information age would also lead to a new set of issues and concomitant initiatives. Robert Morris introduced us to Internet-type incidents before the actual advent of the commercial Internet. Since the Internet itself evolved rather than "started up," that date can be arbitrarily assigned to either 1992, when the registry process was first defined [54], or 1998, when the Internet Corporation for Assigned Names and Numbers took control of its organization [55]. Our view of the Internet concept today rests heavily on the work of Tim Berners–Lee in the development of the hypertext transfer protocol (http) in the same approximate timeframe [56].

7.2 Computer Security and the Growing Internet

By 1992, the number of annual incidents recorded at the CERT/CC had risen from less than 300 in 1989 to around 900 three years later. That baseline number can be contrasted with the almost 4000 incidents that were reported at the end of the 1990s. A rise of over 400% in the succeeding 8 years indicated that computer security was a major issue [57]. In the meantime, the Internet had grown from a minute number of users in 1990 to an astounding 40 million consumers by the end of the decade [57].

If you view the situation from the standpoint of the situation in 2000, you can see that overnight, the technology had practically outpaced anybody's ability to operate it securely. We had 40,000,000 users and the same basic set of security processes and technologies that we had 5 years earlier, when the number of users was in the thousands.

7.3 Organized Incident Response

Given the exponentially rising number of exploits and the growing sophistication of the attackers, something had to be done. In response to the Morris Worm in the late 1980s, the federal government established the CERT/CC to "coordinate communication among experts during security emergencies and to help prevent future incidents" [58]. Thus, the CERT/CC might be considered the first organized response to the problem of Internet incidents, and it has continued to serve in that capacity. However, one of its chief contributions is the development of a formal disciplined process aimed at identifying and mitigating cyber-based incidents.

An organized management security response was a logical outcome of the growth of the commercial Internet. In 1990 and for several years afterward, it might have been acceptable to treat incidents in an ad hoc and reactive manner because there were so few of them, approximately 900 [57]. However, by 1995 the number of incidents had grown to over 2000 and was on its way up to nearly doubling by 1998 [57]. As a consequence, an ad hoc response became impossible, and something more structured was needed.

7.4 Incident Management

The concept that was developed by the CERT/CC was in the form of a defined and fully documented strategy and a set of end-to-end measures. These measures were specifically designed to detect and mitigate incidents from occurrence to resolution. The term that the CERT/CC adopted to describe their new process was "incident management" [58]. Incident management directly coordinates the routine monitoring and detection of incidents as they occur. It follows a defined process that is specifically designed to mitigate the event involving the routine development of [58]:

- policies and procedures that define and assign the appropriate roles and responsibilities for personnel involved in incident management activities;
- equipment, infrastructure, tools, and supporting materials to protect systems, detect suspicious events and incidents, assist in recovery, and support the resumption of operations; and
- qualified staff who are trained to perform consistent, reliable, and high-quality incident management functions.

In essence, incident management is to be embedded as a formal exercise that is integral to the operation of the organization, much as any other routine part of the organization. Incident management has become a routine part of conventional cybersecurity practice because the technology and its threat environment require it. The process itself could probably not have been developed any earlier than 1988. But it was the astounding increase in Internet incidents during the 1990s that gave it the impetus needed to make it a staple in the cybersecurity profession.

7.5 Malware

Carnegie Mellon's CERT/CC and DHS's United States Computer Emergency Readiness Team (US-CERT) [59] are specific examples of societal responses brought on by the increase in Internet incidents that are a consequence of the establishment and development of Internet technologies. In a similar fashion, the massive expansion of the commercial software industry as a result of the newer and much cheaper processing power that was now available, combined with the almost open access of the Internet, created a different but highly related problem during the same time period: malware.

Like many tech-terms, *malware* is simply a combination of two words: "malicious software." Malware is software that might be used to disrupt a computer operation, gather sensitive information, or gain access to private computer systems [60]. If you are a criminal in today's world, malware serves many useful purposes [61]. Malware includes viruses and spyware that can be installed on a computer, phone, or mobile device without consent. They can cause a device to crash and can be used to monitor and control online activity. Criminals can use malware to steal personal information, send spam, and commit fraud [61].

A lot of malware depend on user naiveté. But the most destructive types of malware are designed to exploit defects in the underlying code. These exploits can either attack the operating infrastructure or the applications using the infrastructure. Hence the increasing requirement is for secure software. The security of code became an issue as the number of exploits attacking software defects increased with the advent of the commercial Internet.

When the computer operated in isolation from other computers, it was hard to attack it directly, except through a physical connection, such as an exchange of floppy disks. However, once a machine is connected to other Internet users, it is fair game for every bad actor in cyberspace, and is also exposed to a wide variety of nasty pieces of code like Trojan Horses, rootkits, and back-doors. Most of those severe threats exploit coding issues like buffer overflow and the injection of defects.

7.6 The Need for Defect-Free Software

7.6.1 Build Security In

As a result of the increasing emphasis on the need for defect-free software, the Build Security In (BSI) website was launched in 2005 [62,63]. The BSI Software Assurance Initiative sought to alter the way that software is developed so that it is less vulnerable to attack, and security is "built in" from the start. As part of the initiative, a BSI content catalog has been made available (https://buildsecurityin.us-cert.gov). This catalog is intended to be used by software developers and software development organizations that want information and practical guidance on how to produce secure and reliable software. The catalog is based on the principle that software security is fundamentally a SE problem and must be addressed in a systematic way throughout the software development lifecycle. The catalog contains or links to a broad range of information about best practices, tools, guidelines, rules, principles, and other knowledge to help organizations build secure and reliable software.

7.6.2 CWE Project

The BSI initiative has produced a number of critical outcomes, including Mitre Corporation's Common Weakness Enumeration (CWE) Project [64]. Mitre assembled a clearinghouse to identify and classify any identifiable form of weakness (CWE), or vulnerability (CVE), or attack (CAPEC) on code. A catalog of these items is available to the public [64], and its mission is to continue to track and record those entities as they appear. As attacks on cyber-physical systems grow, there is an effort underway for expansion of information collection into aspects beyond code.

7.7 Summary

BSI and the CWE Project are valuable initiatives because so many Internet-connected organizations need information about software defects that could be attacked. Those attacks were leveraged to exponentially high levels by the fact that computers were now accessible from any place on earth as a result of the Internet. Initiatives would not have taken place in any reasonable volume if it were not for the fact that commercial software of dubious quality had become such a ubiquitous part of our way of life. Thus, initiatives like the CERT/CC, BSI, and the CWE Project rest on a pyramid of technological development, from early programming and communications network development, to mass availability of defect-laden software on an open platform like the Internet.

8. CYBERSECURITY BECOMES A SOCIETAL ISSUE: LEGAL FRAMEWORKS

The issues and concerns associated with security in cyberspace were major societal issues by the mid-2000s. This is evidenced by the passage of two laws. The first of these is the E-Government Act of 2002 (Public Law 107–347, 44 U.S.C. § 101, H.R. 2458/S. 803) [65]; the second law is the Federal Information Security Management Act (FISMA), which was enacted as Title III of the E-Government Act.

8.1 The E-Government Act of 2002

This law was enacted on December 17, 2002 to "enhance the management and promotion of electronic Government services and processes by establishing a Federal Chief Information Officer within the Office of Management and Budget (OMB), and by establishing a broad framework of measures that require using Internet-based information technology to enhance citizen access to Government information and services, and for other purposes" [Introduction, 65].

The E-Government act is a watershed in the discussion of responses to technological change since it did two important things. First and foremost it consolidated what had been, up to that point, ad hoc responses to threats as they arose into a single unified strategy. Second, it gave the force of law to the requirement to deal with threats originating from technological changes. It also formally recognized the importance of information security to the economic and national security interests of the United States.

8.2 Federal Information Security Management Act (FISMA)

Relevant to our discussion, 44 U.S.C. § 3541, the FISMA, was enacted as Title III of the E-Government Act. FISMA requires each federal agency to develop, document, and implement an agency-wide program to provide information security for the information and information systems that support the operations and assets of the agency [66]. FISMA coverage includes those systems provided or managed by another agency, contractor, or other source and emphasizes a "risk-based policy for cost-effective security."

Based on FISMA requirements, agency program officials, chief information officers, and inspectors general (IGs) conduct annual reviews of a federal agency's information security program and report the results to the OMB [63]. This information is evaluated by OMB as part of its oversight responsibilities and includes OMB's annual report to Congress on agency compliance with the act.

FISMA assigns specific responsibilities to federal agencies, the NIST, and the OMB to strengthen information system security [66]. In particular, FISMA requires the head of each agency to implement policies and procedures to cost effectively reduce information technology security risks to an acceptable level [66].

8.2.1 Standards, Guidelines, and Associated Methods and Techniques

As documented in FISMA, the term *information security* means protecting information and information systems from unauthorized access, use, disclosure, disruption, modification, or destruction in order to provide integrity, confidentiality, and availability [66]. To provide adequate information security for all agency operations in accordance with FISMA, NIST is assigned responsibility for developing [66] the following:

- Standards
- Guidelines
- Associated methods and techniques

NIST works closely with federal agencies to improve their understanding and implementation of FISMA. NIST publishes standards and guidelines that provide the foundation for strong information security programs at agencies. NIST performs its statutory responsibilities through the Computer Security Division of the Information Technology Laboratory and develops standards, metrics, tests, and validation programs to promote, measure, and validate the security in information systems and services [66].

NIST hosts the FISMA implementation project, which includes the Information Security Automation Program (ISAP), security content automation protocol (SCAP), and National Vulnerability Database (NVD), which is the US government content repository for ISAP and SCAP. The NVD is the US government repository of standards-based vulnerability management data enabling automation of vulnerability management, security measurement, and compliance [66].

FISMA defines a standard control-process-based framework for managing information security. The FISMA framework must be followed for all information systems used or operated by a US federal government agency or by a contractor or other organization on behalf of a federal agency. This framework is further defined by the standards and guidelines developed by NIST.

According to FISMA requirements, the head of each agency shall develop and maintain an inventory of major information systems (including major national security systems) operated by or under the control of such an agency [66]. The identification of information systems in an inventory under this subsection includes an identification of the interfaces between each such system and all other systems or networks, including those not operated by or under the control of the agency [66].

8.2.2 Security Requirements

Federal information systems must meet the minimum security requirements. These requirements are defined in a mandatory security standard required by the FISMA legislation, FIPS 200 "Minimum Security Requirements for Federal Information and Information Systems" [67]. Organizations must meet the minimum security requirements by selecting the appropriate security controls and assurance requirements as described in NIST Special Publication 800-53, "Recommended Security Controls for Federal Information Systems" [68].

The process of selecting the appropriate security controls and assurance requirements for organizational information systems to achieve adequate security is a multifaceted, risk-based activity. It involves IT management and operational personnel within the organization. Agencies have flexibility in applying the baseline security controls in accordance with the tailoring guidance provided in Special Publication 800-53 [68]. This approach allows agencies to adjust the security controls to more closely fit their mission requirements and operational environments [68].

8.3 Summary

The controls selected or planned must be documented in the System Security Plan [67]. The combination of FIPS 200 and NIST Special Publication 800-53 requires a foundational level of security for all federal information and information systems [67]. The agency's risk assessment validates the security control set and determines if any additional controls are needed to protect agency operations (including mission, functions, image, or reputation), agency assets, individuals, other organizations, or the nation [68]. The resulting set of security controls establishes a level of "security due diligence" for the federal agency and its contractors.

There have been a number of attempts to enhance the response to the threat to the national well-being that is represented by cyberspace. Those attempts include the Cyber Security Act (2010), the International Cybercrime Reporting and Cooperation Act (2010), and the Protecting Cyberspace as a National Asset Act (2010). Nonetheless, FISMA requirements remain the primary Federal mandate for actual response to the issues and concerns that have been raised by the advance of Internet technology.

Although FISMA is still only applicable to systems in the federal sphere, its risk- and standard-best-practice-based approach has served as the basis for many other kinds of response to the growing number of threats raised by the growth of Internet technologies.

9. COMPLEXITY AND SUPPLY CHAINS: THE NEED FOR BROAD-SCALE INTEGRATION

System integration was not invented in the 2000s, but the problems that arise from integrating large systems out of smaller ones were infinitely exacerbated by the rise of the black-hat community after 2000. In 1994, hacking and other kinds of cyberexploits were generally considered to be a hobbyist's domain [69]. To be sure, there were expert hackers in that world, but the black-hat community mainly comprised shadowy figures doing 72-h hacks, while living on Skittles [69].

Ten years later, cyberspace had become very big business for every malicious entity, from hostile nation states and the mob, to teenage entrepreneurs conducting business, which was typically conducted on a street corner or in their parents' basement [69]. Whole websites on the Darkweb are now devoted to selling cracking and hacking tools, along with illegal drugs and contract hit men, and operations like the Russian Business Network (RBN) can build 2 million node botnets with a single virus (Storm) [70]. Nevertheless, the larger problem revolves around the issue of uncontrolled complexity. That is, as the technology advances, the resulting additional complexity in the product and process, which is necessary for creation, also creates a larger number of issues that have to be addressed to assure quality and security.

As we have seen, the need to devise new responses to technological imperatives has been an overall trend since the 1960s. In essence, the growing complexity of programs shaped the need for engineered software. The proliferation of computers in business imposed a concomitant need for security principles and the iniquitousness of computers created the need for large-scale laws and initiatives to address and control their use. None of that evolution in industry practice would have been required if computing had continued to remain in the backrooms where it was developed in the 1950s. But unfortunately the computer is, and always will be, far too powerful a force in society to stay in the background.

9.1 Integrated Complex Applications

Perhaps, the most important issue now facing us is the growing size and complexity of the large-scale programs we have adapted to serve most of society's needs as well as the process that we have adopted to build them. In simple terms, most of today's complex applications are not built, as much as they are "integrated" into highly complex modular arrangements that rival the most complex things built by man. To build something as complex as a military weapons system, the components are normally integrated from the bottom up, under a top-down plan.

This is not a new concept. Bottom-up integration has been the approach of choice since Cheops built his first pyramid. What *is* new is the fact that the components that compose that complex stack are too complex and fundamentally invisible to be clearly understood and managed as individual entities in the product. Also the components come from a vast array of sources and are constructed, validated, and maintained with highly variable processes, practices, and capabilities. An acquirer has very little knowledge of the development practices used for a selected product, and at this time, no public certification of a supplier's practices is available [71]. One example of this variability was shown in the impact of a vulnerability in OpenSSL described in the Heartbleed incident [72].

9.2 Component Complexity and Virtuality

Component complexity and virtuality create the problem that the pieces that go into a technology cannot be realistically monitored and controlled. So we are left with "trust" as the only alternative for assurance.

It might even be possible to trust a product that was built by a well-known and familiar partner. But due to the high cost of onshore development and the "faster–cheaper–better" mentality of just-in-time production, most of the work that goes into building a technology product is outsourced down a supply chain. It is well documented that we have lost all visibility into what is going on at the bottom of that chain [73].

9.3 The Technology Supply Chain

The lack of ability to ensure the resilience and security of the technology supply chain has opened up a significant avenue of attack for any bad actor seeking to subvert everyday life in any technologically advanced country. In the United States, we build critical infrastructure out of components that are derived from global sources. Thus, it would be an easy matter for a foreign nation state, terrorist group, or even an individual to compromise a purportedly secure critical system through a third- or fourth-tier supplier situated in a country that is out of sight and control of the prime contractor [73].

9.3.1 Risks to Critical Infrastructure

Moreover, because of the complexity of the supply chain, nobody knows for sure whether the parts that constitute our critical infrastructure (1) are actually what they were intended to be, (2) whether they are counterfeit, or (3) if they contain maliciously inserted objects [74]. Members of Congress determined [75] that the vulnerabilities created by insecure ICT supply chains would have to be addressed if we ever wanted to be certain that our adversaries cannot, "destroy power grids, water, and sanitary services; induce mass flooding; release toxic/radioactive materials; or bankrupt any business by inserting malicious objects into the (ICT) components that comprise our infrastructure" [76].

Because of the potential critical impact of insecure supply chains on the US infrastructure, ICT Supply Chain Risk Management (SCRM) has been placed on an annual "Key Issues, High Risk" list (2013) [77]. A major reason for growing concern focused on supply chain risk derives from the fact that most systems today are integrated from existing elements (eg, legacy, COTS, open source, and freeware). Business justifies integration because it can get the same functionality for 10 cents on a dollar of what it would cost to build it themselves. The parts are obtained through a vast, global ICT supply chain. In effect, most of our products are composed of items from all over the world: software comes from India, chips and programmed logic come from Korea, and small components come from Vietnam and China. Poorly managed ICT supply chains pose a major security threat to the national infrastructure [77].

At its core, the challenge lies in assuring the integrity of disparate objects as they move from lower level construction to higher level integration. There are a number of levels of parent–child relationships involved in a supply chain, and the number of those levels varies depending on the complexity of the product [73]. Nonetheless, each element in the supply chain has to satisfy the explicit purpose that defined its placement in the development hierarchy [73].

9.3.2 Supply Chain Risk Management (SCRM)

In 2010 the US government, through the development of a NIST standard, established a set of best practices for formal SCRM (NIST SP 800-161). This standard was a 2-year effort to assemble available Federal SCRM knowledge through a collaboration of NIST, DHA, and DoD, and design a means to at least define what constitutes proper SCRM practice for the workforce [78]. Ensuring a complex, distributed process like a supply chain requires a coordinated set of standard, consistently executed activities to enforce the requisite visibility and control into the process. In that respect, the locus of control for SCRM is in the process rather than the product itself, since the actual product is either too complex or virtual [79]. Yet, because the development process is usually occurring in a number of global locations, typically at the same time, the requisite level of understanding and control is hard to achieve [79].

Thus, the aim is to address supply chain assurance problems by "providing a consistent, disciplined environment for developing the product, assessing what could go wrong in the process (ie, assessing risks), determining which risks to address (ie, setting mitigation priorities), implementing actions to address high-priority risks and bringing those risks within tolerance" [80]. In the latest revision (rev 4) of NIST 800-53, Assessing Security and Privacy Controls in Federal Information Systems and Organizations, initially released February 28, 2012, existing security controls were augmented to include SCRM as appropriate. Because this is a global issue, many major commercial organizations were concerned that they would be faced with different compliance requirements in each country where they did business. This concern has been addressed through the development of an international standard ISO/IEC 27036, Information Security for Supplier Relationships. Creators of the NIST 800-161 contributed extensively to the development and finalization of the international effort.

There is still much work remaining to embed SCRM practices into the typical acquisition lifecycle. On the educational side, the SwA Body of Knowledge (BOK) [81] can be extended to develop new processes to monitor and control production and integration activity in multiple simultaneous sites [79]. The SwA curriculum recommendations [82–86] can be used to provide the education needed to support effective practice. Much of this work fits with the advice in NIST 800-53(4) [68].

9.4 Summary

The response to insecure supply chains has built on the knowledge and best practices of SwA in development and design, but there is an added complexity of controlling the results since the acquirer and supplier are in separate organizations. Requirements must be communicated through the acquisition process and results evaluated based on information provided by the supplier organization.

The size and complexity of the applications and the approach to program construction in the year 2014 has created an environment where conventional ideas about how to build software have been replaced by new paradigms. Likewise, those new paradigms on the supply side demand a response from the profession that was not necessary 10 years ago, but which is essential now.

10. WHERE WE ARE NOW

As it has done a number of times in the past, the government has been a visible participant in the response. Over the past 50 years, the field of cyber emerged from the backroom of researchers and hobbyists, where it first resided due to the relatively exotic nature of the technology, to become the prime facilitator of our way of life.

Consumers stepped into the field buying technology gadgets and mobile devices for games, communication, and photography. Consumer services linking Facebook and Google emerged. Manufacturing, banking, mining, and other industries, including utilities and other critical infrastructure, capitalized on the flexibility and process improvement capabilities of software. Because of its centrality to our society as a whole, cyber has become much more of a social and political issue.

The Northeast power failure of 2003 was initially thought to be a cyber-attack, but turned out to be an inevitable result of poorly designed interfaces and interdependencies with insufficient resiliency to handle an abnormal condition [87]. It was probably little comfort to the victims of the outage that a similar problem had occurred in 1965 as the result of human error in performing a maintenance activity. The response to new challenges has been much more comprehensive and societal in its general impetus and form. That is because computers and computing have a profound influence on every aspect of our society. The volume of computing capability is privately owned [88], requiring a public–private partnership to ensure our way of life.

Issues arising out of the appearance of new concerns that are the outcome of technological advances are more likely to involve contextual strategic policy and managerial actions, rather than simply being dealt with as a scientific exercise. The actual science of computing might have been the one-stop-shop for the solution of cyber concerns in the days when computers were not so critical to our national existence. Nevertheless, history has shown that the advance of computing as a field and profession will create the need to ensure that unsafe technological progress is not the eventual source of our demise.

Recent legislative efforts provide indicators that US citizens are responding to the attacks and other cyber issues that have been front-page news by structuring control mandates and levying restrictions to establish a higher degree of SwA. One survey reported over 47% of US adults have had their personal information exposed. The *Critical Code: Software Producibility for Defense* report noted that software is essential to all aspects of military system capabilities and operations. In 1960, software handled 8% of the F-4 Phantom fighter functionality; it expanded to 45% of the F-16 Fighting Falcon in 1982 and to 80% of the F-22 Raptor in 2000 [89]. This software is riddled with security weaknesses similar to those plaguing consumers. The growing concern for software security was communicated to the DoD through a section in the 2013 National Defense Appropriation Act (NDAA) mandating a commitment to SwA [90] resulting in policy and acquisition restructuring. The President signed the Cybersecurity Enhancement Act of 2014 on December 18, 2014 [91]. This law provides for an ongoing, voluntary, public–private partnership to improve cybersecurity, including workforce development and education, and public awareness and preparedness.

The *Critical Code: Software Producibility for Defense* report also noted the shortage of personnel with the software expertise to meet the needs for mission-critical software-intensive programs [89]. Software developer expertise has been reported in short supply internationally [92]. Federal agencies have responded to this need through programs such as the CE21 program [93] with goals to

• increase the number and diversity of K-14 students and teachers who develop and practice computational competencies in a variety of contexts and

• increase the number and diversity of early postsecondary students who are engaged and have the background in computing necessary to successfully pursue degrees in computing-related and computationally intensive fields of study.

Unfortunately, there does not appear to be an equally broad educational effort to address cybersecurity. No federal programs exist at this time to fund increased cybersecurity education and software developers are not required to meet any knowledge level of cybersecurity expertise to create and implement or update existing software. As a result, it seems likely that the pace of things will follow the same trajectory as it has for the past 30 years. That is, some technological breakthrough will trigger a large-scale response from the society as a whole and government in particular, which will seek to ensure that the advance is properly focused for the good of mankind.

ACKNOWLEDGMENTS

This material is based upon work funded and supported by the Department of Defense under Contract No. FA8721-05-C-0003 with CMU for the operation of the SEI, a federally funded research and development center.

REFERENCES

[1] N.R. Mead, Software engineering education: how far we've come and how far we have to go, J. Syst. Softw. 82 (4) (2009) 571–575, http://dx.doi.org/10.1016/j.jss2008.12.038. http://www.sciencedirect.com/science/article/pii/S0164121208002756. accessed August 2015.
[2] C. Böhm, G. Jacopini, Flow diagrams, turing machines and languages with only two formation rules, Commun. ACM 9 (5) (1966) 366–371.
[3] P. Naur, B. Randell, Report on a conference sponsored by the NATO Science Committee, (October 1968) Garmisch, Germany.
[4] E.W. Dijkstra, Letters to the editor: go to statement considered harmful, Commun. ACM 11 (3) (1968) 147–148.

[5] R.C. Linger, H.D. Mills, B.I. Witt, Structured Programming: Theory and Practice, Addison-Wesley, Reading, MA, 1979.

[6] J. Backus, The History of FORTRAN I, II, and III, History of Programming Languages, Association for Computing Machinery, New York, NY, 1981.

[7] J.W. Backus, F.L. Bauer, J. Green, C. Katz, J. McCarthy, P. Naur, A.J. Perlis, H. Rutishauser, K. Samuelson, B. Vauquois, J.H. Wegstein, A. van Wijngaarden, M. Woodger, Revised Report on the Algorithmic Language Algol 60, IFIP TC 2 on Programming Languages, (August 1962).

[8] P. Naur, Report on the algorithmic language ALGOL 60, Commun. ACM 3 (5) (1960) 299–314.

[9] A. Ferguson, A History of Computer Programming Languages, Brown University, New York, NY, 2004. http://cs.brown.edu/~adf/programming_languages.html. accessed August 2015.

[10] McGraw-Hill Staff, McGraw-Hill Encyclopedia of Science and Technology, 2009. p.454. New York, NY.

[11] E.D. Reilly, Milestones in Computer Science and Information Technology, Greenwood Publishing Group, Westport, CT, ISBN: 978-1-57356-521-9, 2003, pp. 156–157.

[12] R. Linger, C. Trammell, Cleanroom software engineering reference, Technical Report CMU/SEI-96-TR-022, Software Engineering Institute, Carnegie Mellon University, 1996. accessed August 2015, http://resources.sei.cmu.edu/library/asset-view.cfm? AssetID=12635.

[13] R.E. Fairley, Software Engineering Concepts, McGraw Hill, New York, NY, 1984.

[14] J.C.R. Licklider, Man–Computer Symbiosis, IRE Trans. Hum. Factors Electron. HFE-1 (1960) 4–11.

[15] L. Earnest, J. Wong, P. Edwards, Vigilance and Vacuum Tubes: The SAGE System 1956–63, Transcript of public lecture given on May 19, 1998, The Computer Museum History Center, Moffett Field, Mountain View, CA, 1998. accessed August 2015, http://ed-thelen.org/Sage-Talk.html.

[16] R. Serling, Eagle, St. Martin's/Marek, New York, NY, 1985. p. 347.

[17] J.C.R. Licklider, Memorandum for Members and Affiliates of the Intergalactic Computer Network, Kurzweil Technologies, Wellesley, MA, 2001. http://www.kurzweilai.net/memorandum-for-members-and-affiliates-of-the-intergalactic-computer-network. Accessed May 2016.

[18] J. Abbate, Inventing the Internet, MIT Press, Cambridge, 2000.

[19] B.M. Leiner, V.G. Cerf, D.D. Clark, R.E. Kahn, L. Kleinrock, D.C. Lynch, J. Postel, L.G. Roberts, S. Wolff, A Brief History of Internet, The Internet Society, Wellesley, MA, 2003. http://www.internetsociety.org/internet/what-internet/history-internet/brief-history-internet. Accessed May 2016.

[20] J.H. Saltzer, M.D. Schroeder, The protection of information in computer systems, Proc. IEEE 63 (9) (1975) 1278–1308. http://citeseer.ist.psu.edu/viewdoc/summary? doi=10.1.1.126.9257. Accessed May 2016.

[21] R.E. Smith, A contemporary look at Saltzer and Schroeder's 1975 design principles, IEEE Secur. Priv. 10 (6) (2012) 20–25.

[22] D. Price, Blind whistling phreaks and the FBI's historical reliance on phone tap criminality, CounterPunch 30 (2008). http://www.counterpunch.org/2008/06/30/blind-whistling-phreaks-and-the-fbi-s-historical-reliance-on-phone-tap-criminality. Accessed August 2015.

[23] Committee on National Security Systems, National information assurance (IA) glossary, CNSS Instruction No. 4009, April 26, 2010. National Counterintelligence and Security Center, Washington, D.C., 2010. https://www.ncsc.gov/nittf/docs/CNSSI-4009_National_Information_Assurance.pdf. Assessed May 2016.

[24] C. Woody, N. Mead, D. Shoemaker, Foundations for Software Assurance, in: Proceedings of the 45th IEEE Hawaii International Conference on System Sciences, 2013. HICSS 2012, Pittsburgh, PA, 5368–5374, January 4, 2012–January 7, 2012. http://resources.sei.cmu.edu/library/asset-view.cfm?assetid=75631. Accessed May 2016.

[25] E.E. Keet, A personal recollection of software's early days (1960–1979): Part 2, IEEE Ann. Hist. Comput. 27 (4) (October/December 2005) 31–45. Los Alamitos, CA, http://www.vanguardatlantic.com/Annals Article Part 2.pdf. Assessed May 2016.

[26] N. Ravo, E. Nash, The evolution of cyberpunk, New York Times August 8 (1993). http://www.nytimes.com/1993/08/08/style/the-evolution-of-cyberpunk.html. accessed August 2015.

[27] F. Cohen, Computer Viruses: Theory and Experiments. IFIP/Sec '84. Computer Security: A Global Challenge, Proceedings of the Second IFIP International Conference on Computer Security (2006) 143–158. Kluwer, Boston, MA, http://www.facweb.iitkgp.ernet.in/~shamik/spring2006/i&ss/papers/ComputerVirusesTheoryandExperiments.pdf. Accessed May 2016.

[28] Security News, What is a Virus in the Wild?, Symantec Corporation, Mountain View, CA, 2015. http://www.pctools.com/security-news/virus-in-the-wild. Accessed August 2015.

[29] Eugene Spafford, The Internet worm program: an analysis, Purdue Technical Report CSD-TR-823, Purdue University, 1988. http://spaf.cerias.purdue.edu/tech-reps/823. pdf. accessed August 2015.

[30] S. Eltringham (Ed.), Prosecuting Computer Crimes, Computer Crime and Intellectual Property Section, Criminal Division, Office of Legal Education, Executive Office for United States Attorneys, in: 2013. http://www.justice.gov/sites/default/files/criminal-ccips/legacy/2015/01/14/ccmanual.pdf. accessed August 2015.

[31] R. Hauben, From the ARPANET to the Internet, TCP Digest (UUCP) (2015). http://www.columbia.edu/~rh120/other/tcpdigest_paper.txt. accessed August 2015.

[32] NSFNET, The Partnership that Changed the World an Event Celebrating 20 Years of Internet Invention and Progress. National Science Foundation, Arlington, VA, 2007. November 29–30. http://www.nsfnet-legacy.org/NSFNET_ProgramBook. pdf. Accessed May 2016.

[33] R.D. Pethia, 20+ Years of cyber (in) security, SEI Webinar Series, Software Engineering Institute, Carnegie Mellon University, Pittsburgh, PA, 2013. http://www.sei.cmu.edu/webinars/view_webinar.cfm?webinarid=59067. Accessed May 2016.

[34] P.J. Friedl, SCAMP: the missing link in the PC's past? PC Mag. 2 (6) (1983) 190–191.

[35] R. Sipe (Editor-in-Chief), Fusion, transfusion or confusion/future directions in computer entertainment, Computer Gaming World 77, (December 1990) 26–28, http://www.cgwmuseum.org/galleries/issues/cgw_77.pdf. Accessed August 2015.

[36] Gartner Inc., Gartner Says Worldwide Software Market Grew 4.8 Percent in 2013, Gartner Inc., Stamford, CT, 2013. http://www.gartner.com/newsroom/id/2696317. Accessed August 2015.

[37] Standish Group, the Standish Group Report. CHAOS. Project Smart, The Standish Group, Boston, MA, (2014). https://www.projectsmart.co.uk/white-papers/chaos-report.pdf. Accessed May 2016.

[38] C. Jones, Software Quality in 2013: A survey of the state of the art, Namcook Analytics, LLC, Narragansett, RI, 2013. http://namcookanalytics.com/wp-content/uploads/2013/10/SQA2013Long.pdf. Accessed May 2016.

[39] W. Humphrey, A Discipline for Software Engineering, Addison-Wesley, Boston, MA, 1994.

[40] Software Engineering Institute, Statistics and History, Carnegie Mellon University, Pittsburgh, PA. http://www.sei.cmu.edu/about/statisticshistory.cfm. Accessed August 2015.

[41] N. Hall, J. Miklos, Formal education within the software life cycle, in: R. Fairley, P. Freeman (Eds.), Issues in Software Engineering Education, Springer-Verlag, New York, NY, 1989.

[42] D.J. Bagert, X. Mu, Current state of software engineering master's degree programs in the United States, in: Proc. 35th Annual Conference, Frontiers in Education Conference, IEEE Computer Society Press, October 19, 2005–October 22, 2005. F1G-1–F1G-6. http://ieeexplore.ieee.org/stamp/stamp.jsp? arnumber=1612026. Assessed May 2016.

[43] W.S. Humphrey, Characterizing the software process: a maturity framework. Technical Report CMU/SEI-87-TR-11, June 1987, (2015) http://www.sei.cmu.edu/reports/87tr011.pdf. Accessed August 2015.

[44] W.S. Humphrey, Managing the Software Process, Addison-Wesley, Boston, MA, 1989.

[45] M.C. Paulk, C.V. Weber, B. Curtis, M.B. Chrissis, The capability maturity model: guidelines for improving the software process, SEI Series in Software Engineering, Addison-Wesley, Reading, MA, 1995.

[46] Joint Taskforce for Computing Curricula, Software Engineering 2004: Curricular Guidelines for Undergraduate Programs in Software Engineering, IEEE Computer Society, Los Alamitos, CA, 2004.

[47] M. Lutz, RIT offers nation's first undergraduate degree in software engineering, Forum Adv. Softw. Eng. Ed. 6 (14) (1996). http://tab.computer.org/fase/fase-archive/v6/v6n14.txt. Accessed August 2015.

[48] IEEE Computer Society, SWEBOK Overview, IEEE Computer Society, Los Alamitos, CA, 2008. SE Online.

[49] IEEE Computer Society, Software Engineering Code of Ethics and Professional Practice, IEEE Computer Society, Los Alamitos, CA, 1999. https://www.acm.org/about/se-code. Accessed August 2015.

[50] N.R. Mead, Issues in licensing and certification of software engineers, in: Proceedings of the 10th Conf. Software Eng. Ed. and Training, IEEE Computer Society Press, Los Alamitos, CA, 1997, pp. 150–160.

[51] N.R. Mead, Are we going to fish or cut bait? Licensing and certification of software professionals, Cutter IT J. 11 (5) (1998) 4–8.

[52] N.R. Mead, A.J. Turner, Current accreditation, certification, and licensure activities related to software engineering, Ann. Softw. Eng. 6 (1998) 167–180.

[53] IEEE Computer Society, CSDP: Certified Software Development Professional, IEEE Computer Society, Los Alamitos, CA, 2008. http://www2.computer.org/portal/web/certification/about. Accessed August 2015.

[54] E. Gerich, RFC 1366. Guidelines for Management of IP Address Space, MERIT Systems, Internet Engineering Task Force, Internet Society, Reston, VA, http://www.rfc-editor.org/rfc/rfc1366.txt. Accessed August 2015.

[55] National Telecommunications and Information Administration, Management of Internet Names and Addresses, Fed. Regist. 63 (111) (1998) 31741–31751. http://www.ntia.doc.gov/files/ntia/publications/6_5_98dns.txt. Accessed August 2015.

[56] T. Berniers-Lee, M. Fischetti, Weaving the Web: The Original Design and Ultimate Destiny of the World Wide Web, HarperCollins, New York, NY, 1999. http://www.w3.org/People/Berners-Lee/Weaving/Overview.html. Accessed August 2015.

[57] B. Fraser, Computer Security Incident and Vulnerability Trends, CERT, Software Engineering Institute, Carnegie Mellon University, Pittsburgh, PA, 1999. www.stonesoup.org/meetings/9905/secorg.pres/fraser.pdf. Accessed August 2015.

[58] G. Killcrece, Incident Management, Build-Security-In, Carnegie Mellon University, Pittsburgh, PA, 2013. https://buildsecurityin.us-cert.gov/articles/best-practices/incident-management/incident-management#footnote1_738ypgx. Accessed August 2015.

[59] Department of Homeland Security, US-CERT Infosheet Version 2, https://www.us-cert.gov/sites/default/files/publications/infosheet_US-CERT_v2.pdf. Accessed August 2015.

[60] Techterms, Malware, http://www.techterms.com/definition/malware. Accessed August 2015.

[61] Federal Trade Commission, Consumer Information, Malware, http://www.consumer.ftc.gov/articles/0011-malware. Accessed August 2014.

[62] Department of Homeland Security, https://buildsecurityin.us-cert.gov. Accessed August 2015.

[63] G. McGraw, Software Security: Building Security In. Software Security, Addison-Wesley, Boston, MA, 2006.

[64] The Mitre Corporation, Common Weakness Enumeration, http://cwe.mitre.org, 2015. Accessed August 2015.

[65] U.S. Government, E-Government Act of 2002, 2002. http://www.gpo.gov/fdsys/pkg/PLAW-107publ347/html/PLAW-107publ347.htm. Accessed August 2015.

[66] National Institute of Standards and Technology (NIST), FISMA, Detailed Overview, http://csrc.nist.gov/groups/SMA/fisma/overview.html, Updated, April 2014. Accessed August 2015.

[67] National Institute of Standards and Technology, NIST Special Publication 800-53 Revision 4, Security and Privacy Controls for Federal Information Systems and Organizations, (April 2013) http://csrc.nist.gov/publications/fips/fips200/FIPS-200-final-march.pdf. Accessed August 2015.

[68] Computer Security Division, Information Technology Laboratory, NIST Special Publication 800-53 Revision 4, Security and Privacy Controls for Federal Information Systems and Organizations, National Institute of Standards and Technology, (March 2006) http://csrc.nist.gov/publications/fips/fips200/FIPS-200-final-march.pdf. Accessed August 2014.

[69] D. Shoemaker, D.B. Kennedy, Criminal profiling and cybercriminal investigations, in: M. Pittaro, F. Schmalleger (Eds.), Crimes of the Internet, Prentice-Hall, Upper Saddle River, NJ, 2009, pp. 456–476.

[70] R. Vamosi, Looking inside the Storm worm botnet, CNET Security, http://www.cnet.com/news/looking-inside-the-storm-worm-botnet, 2008. Accessed August 2012.

[71] R. Ellison, C. Alberts, R. Creel, A. Dorofee, C. Woody, Software Supply Chain Risk Management: From Products to Systems of Systems, CMU/SEI-2010-TN-026, Software Engineering Institute, Carnegie Mellon University, 2010. http://resources.sei.cmu.edu/library/asset-view.cfm?AssetID=9377. Accessed August 2015.

[72] Wikipedia, Heartbleed, http://en.wikipedia.org/wiki/Heartbleed. Accessed August 2015.

[73] United States Government Accountability Office, IT Supply Chain: National Security-Related Agencies Need to Better Address Risks, GAO Report to Congressional Requesters, 2012. March 23, 2012.

[74] D. Goldman, Fake tech gear has infiltrated the U.S. government, CNN Money (2012) http://money.cnn.com/2012/11/08/technology/security/counterfeit-tech/index.html. Accessed August 2015.

[75] House of Representatives, 112th Congress, Committee on Energy and Commerce, Hearing before the Subcommittee on Oversight and Investigations, IT Supply Chain Security: Review of Government and Industry Efforts, Government Printing Office, 2012.

[76] R.A. Clark, H.A. Schmidt, A National Strategy to Secure Cyberspace, The President's Critical Infrastructure Protection Board, Washington, DC, 2003. https://www.us-cert.gov/sites/default/files/publications/cyberspace_strategy.pdf. Accessed August 2015.

[77] General Accounting Office, Key Issues High Risk List, 2013. http://www.gao.gov/highrisk/overview. Accessed August 2015.

[78] J. Boyens, C. Paulsen, R. Moorthy, N. Bartol, S.A. Shankles, NIST Special Publication 800-161: Supply Chain Risk Management Practices for Federal Information Systems and Organizations Computer Security Division, Information Technology Laboratory, 2013.

[79] D. Shoemaker, N. Mead, Building a body of knowledge for ICT supply chain risk management, Crosstalk J. Def. Softw. Eng. 16 (2013). https://buildsecurityin.us-cert. gov/articles/software-assurance-education/building-body-knowledge-ict-supply-chain-risk-management. Accessed August 2015.

[80] A. Dorofee, C. Woody, C. Alberts, R. Creel, R.J. Ellison, A Systemic Approach for Assessing Software Supply-Chain Risk, Carnegie Mellon University, 2014. https:// buildsecurityin.us-cert.gov/articles/best-practices/acquisition/a-systemic-approach-assessing-software-supply-chain-risk. Accessed August 2015.

[81] S. Redwine, Software Assurance, The Common Body of Knowledge to Develop, Sustain and Acquire Software, Build Security In, 2007. https://buildsecurityin.us-cert.gov/resources/dhs-software-assurance-resources/software-assurance-cbk-principles-organization. Accessed August 2015.

[82] N.R. Mead, J. Allen, M. Ardis, T. Hilburn, A. Kornecki, R. Linger, J. McDonald, Software Assurance Curriculum Project Volume I: Master of Software Assurance Reference Curriculum, CMU/SEI-2010-TR-005, Software Engineering Institute, Carnegie Mellon University, Pittsburgh, PA, 2010.

[83] N.R. Mead, T. Hilburn, R. Linger, Software Assurance Curriculum Project Volume II: Undergraduate Course Outlines, CMU/SEI-2010-TR-019, Software Engineering Institute, Carnegie Mellon University, Pittsburgh, PA, 2010.

[84] N.R. Mead, M. Ardis, E. Hawthorne, Software Assurance Curriculum Project Volume IV: Community College Education, CMU/SEI-2011-TR-017, Software Engineering Institute, Carnegie Mellon University, Pittsburgh, PA, 2011. http://resources.sei.cmu.edu/library/asset-view.cfm?assetid=10009. Accessed August 2015.

[85] N.R. Mead, J. Allen, M. Ardis, T. Hilburn, A. Kornecki, R. Linger, Software Assurance Curriculum Project Volume III: Master of Software Assurance Course Syllabi, CMU/SEI-2011-TR-013, Software Engineering Institute, Carnegie Mellon University, Pittsburgh, PA, 2011. http://resources.sei.cmu.edu/library/asset-view.cfm?assetid=9981. Accessed August 2015.

[86] D. Shoemaker, N.R. Mead, J. Ingalsbe, Integrating the Master of Software Assurance Reference Curriculum into the Model Curriculum and Guidelines for Graduate Degree Programs in Information Systems, CMU/SEI-2011-TN-004. Software Engineering Institute, Carnegie Mellon University, Pittsburgh, PA, 2011. http://resources.sei.cmu.edu/library/asset-view.cfm?assetid=9791. Accessed August 2015.

[87] S. Deffree, Northeast blackout leaves 50 M people without power, 2003. http://www.edn.com/electronics-blogs/edn-moments/4394019/Northeast-blackout-leaves-50M-people-without-power--August-14--2003. Accessed August 2015.

[88] Critical Infrastructure Protection Partnerships and Information Sharing, http://www.dhs.gov/critical-infrastructure-protection-partnerships-and-information-sharing. Accessed August 2015.

[89] Computer Science and Telecommunications Board (CSTB), Critical Code: Software Producibility for Defense, National Academies Press, Washington, DC, 2010. p. 19.

ABOUT THE AUTHORS

Dan Shoemaker is a Professor and Director of the Masters of Science in Cyber Security Program at the Center for Cyber Security and Intelligence Studies, a National Security Agency (NSA) Center of Academic Excellence, at the University of Detroit Mercy. Dr. Shoemaker is a well-known speaker and writer in the area of cybersecurity. He has coauthored seven professional books in the fields of Software Engineering and Cybersecurity. His PhD is from the University of Michigan, in Ann Arbor.

Dr. Carol Woody is the Technical Manager of the CERT Cyber Security Engineering team at the Software Engineering Institute (SEI). Her team addresses research for software security and survivability throughout the development and acquisition lifecycles of highly complex networked systems and systems of systems. Dr. Woody has been a senior member of the SEI technical staff since 2001. Her research focuses on building capabilities to address measurement, management, and acquisition for engineering software to provide effective operational cyber security. She holds a BS in Mathematics from the College of William & Mary, an MBA. with distinction from Wake Forest University, and a PhD in Information Systems from NOVA Southeastern University.

Nancy R. Mead is a Fellow and Principal Researcher at the Software Engineering Institute (SEI). Mead is also an Adjunct Professor of Software Engineering at Carnegie Mellon University. She is currently involved in the study of security requirements engineering and the development of software assurance curricula. Mead has more than 150 publications and invited presentations. She is a Fellow of the Institute of Electrical and Electronic Engineers, Inc. (IEEE) and a Distinguished Member of the Association for Computing Machinery (ACM). Dr. Mead received her PhD in mathematics from the Polytechnic Institute of New York, and received a BA and an MS in Mathematics from New York University.

CHAPTER TWO

Privacy Challenges and Goals in mHealth Systems

F. Rahman*, I.D. Addo*, S.I. Ahamed*, J.-J. Yang[†], Q. Wang[†]
*Marquette University, Milwaukee, WI, United States
[†]Research Institute of Information Technology, Tsinghua University, Beijing, PR China

Contents

Abstract

The global phenomena of mobile technology have encouraged collaborations between national governments and diverse international stakeholders in applying mobile-based health (mHealth) solutions as a powerful opportunity for improving health and development in rural and remote areas. A significant impact offered by modern mHealth technologies includes the potential to transform various aspects of healthcare, improving accessibility, quality, and affordability. Over the years, mHealth has become important in the field of healthcare information technology as patients begin to use mobile-based medical sensors to record their daily activities and vital signs. The rapid expansion of mobile information and communications technologies within health service delivery and public health systems has created a range of new opportunities to deliver new forms of interactive health services to patients, clinicians, and

47

caregivers alike. The scope and scale of mHealth interventions range from simple direct-to-individual consumer and interactive patient-provider communications to more complex computer-based systems facilitating coordinated patient care and management.

ABBREVIATIONS

EMRs electronic medical records
HIPAA Health Insurance Portability and Accountability Act
mHealth mobile health
PDP packet data protocol

1. INTRODUCTION

More often than not, the quality of accessible healthcare is an important aspect to determining the quality of life of people worldwide. Mobile health (mHealth) can be defined as the emerging mobile communications and network technologies for healthcare systems. One of the key issues with current-state mHealth applications is an immature understanding of how to effectively implement them. There are a number of rapidly expanding mHealth applications available today particularly on smartphones. Invariably, the proliferation of mHealth applications with minimal integration is not particularly helpful for patients or the general public. Contemporary mHealth practices that make use of mobile phones include various forms of telemedicine, electronic medical records (EMRs), health informatics, and evidence-based medicine [1]. Mobile devices are used to capture and analyze the information gathered from patients and to communicate this information to health practitioners. In some specific cases, physiological data is collected using sensors that may be attached to the patient's body. Body area networks offer an emerging implementation of mHealth solutions.

There are several challenges associated with introducing numerous sensors in a system that is susceptible to security and privacy threats. In some types of systems, sensors are normally the initiators of the mHealth link where body-emitted parameters (eg, heart pulse, blood oxygen level, blood glucose level) are captured, digitized, and transmitted to mobile phones using one or more of the following network communication technologies (eg, Bluetooth, Bluetooth Low Energy (BT-LE), and "ZigBee") [2]. An inherent data collector is usually responsible for capturing and aggregating the received data, performing analysis and characterization, and subsequently transmitting the information to the cloud through cellular technology (eg, using a third- or fourth-generation mobile network "3G" and "4G") [1].

In the scenario captured in Fig. 1 (below), a patient's physical activity (in support of a health and wellness treatment) is being monitored via a multi-modal source consisting of a Wristband tracker and an eyewear device (eg, Google Glass). Both devices have multiple sensors that aid in the data collection process. The aggregate data are transmitted to the smartphone device through the Bluetooth technology. The smartphone, in turn, makes use of a 4G cellular network to transmit the data over the Internet to a remote cloud storage location for further analysis.

The focus of this chapter is to study the challenges and goals in ensuring privacy when sensitive private data is collected by sensors and are transferred to a mobile device or a cloud hosting location for further processing.

Continual monitoring of biometrics-based health information using sensors can result in a collection of very detailed and frequent data over a long period of time. In addition to biometrics information, sensors are capable of collecting data about other private factors of a patients' life, including environment, daily activities, and location. Furthermore, other nonmedical

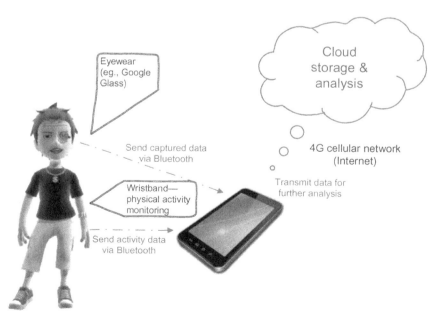

Fig. 1 Sample logical architecture for physical activity monitoring.

applications on the mobile device can collect other types of information about a patient's activities and interests, such as: financial, commerce, diet, and more. Moreover, mobile devices enable a broad range of applications which may gain access to the health data and are capable of sharing the data through third-party applications, such as: healthcare provider, insurance companies, drug manufacturers, and tool provider. Some of the powerful capabilities of smartphones, if not appropriately investigated and restricted, can be used to collect contextually rich data from the sensors and applications, which may result in extracting personally identifiable information (PII). In some cases, this data can be used for other reasons without a patient's consent. Hence, more comprehensive frameworks need to be developed to ensure medical information privacy at various levels and contexts. A high-quality mHealth system should protect privacy and data integrity, remain available, and be auditable.

In 1996, the Health Insurance Portability and Accountability Act (HIPAA) [3] was enacted in the United States. One major regulation of this act is to increase the privacy protection of patients' medical records against unauthorized usage and disclosure. Hospitals, health insurance, publishing organizations, and other entities are asked to comply with the regulations mentioned by the HIPAA. Similar regulations have been proposed and enacted in many countries in the world. To be compliant with the HIPAA, all the mHealth applications, systems, and services need to ensure privacy for patients and end-users.

Many approaches have been proposed over the years, to ensure end-user privacy and help medical institutions or participants comply with those privacy protection regulations. These approaches cover quite a lot of research areas. The implementation of privacy protection techniques during the data publishing phase is quite common and they often attempt to protect patient privacy by transforming the healthcare data before it is shared. Privacy-preserving data publishing models (including, k-anonymity and l-diversity) [4,19], along with privacy-preserving data mining models and methods (like privacy-preserving decision tree and privacy-preserving associate rule mining) [5] have been developed as a result of several research works. In most cases, deidentifying the user or patient in question is the norm. In other scenarios, the goal is to surface aggregate data about users so it is difficult to single out individual users. Sometimes database design approaches are employed to support private data aggregation and inference protection.

Allowing authorized access to sensitive private information is another growing research area. In recent times, several access control models have been developed to increase the flexibility of private data management [6,7]. Privacy-preserving data storage in cloud platforms has attracted quite a lot of attention in recent years [8]. Approaches for privacy-aware data storage and auditing in the cloud environment have been proposed to protect private data [9,10]. Despite all the successes these existing approaches have had, none of them in their entirety, address all the needs and requirements of emerging mHealth solutions. This chapter focuses on investigating the challenges and goals to preserve privacy in mHealth systems or applications. More specifically, we seek to unearth avenues where privacy-preserving approaches can be used effectively, their limitations, and implementation approaches.

2. TECHNOLOGIES USED IN mHealth

Many types of mobile technologies can be utilized for mHealth interventions, ranging from smartphones (hardware and software), laptops, tablets, and mobile-enabled diagnostic, and monitoring devices to devices with mobile alert systems. Devices vary widely in capabilities, price, and strength of evidence that they may improve patient outcomes, workflow efficiencies, and access to health information.

3. MAJOR PRIVACY CHALLENGES

3.1 Privacy Challenges While Using Radio Frequency Identification in mHealth Application

With the deployment and use of radio frequency identification (RFID) technology in the healthcare domain, there are increasing privacy concerns regarding the technical designs of RFID systems. Smart patient tracking, real-time smart asset tracking, improved efficiencies, and improved patient outcomes are only a few of the potential benefits of RFID-based mHealth solutions. However, these benefits are often accompanied by threats of privacy violations [11]. These threats pertain to the potential risks of unauthorized data access, misuse of patient data, and the capabilities of permanently saving and linking information about individuals through temporal and spatial extension of data collection activities. An unauthorized reader without the victim's knowledge can read RFID tags, since it can be read by radio frequency signal. While RFID technology can improve the overall quality of mHealth service delivery, the benefits must be balanced with the privacy and security concerns [18].

The use of RFID introduces a new set of risks. Security risks are associated with the possible failure of the RFID system under various security attacks. For example, uninvited tracking, eavesdropping, and denial of service activities introduce a security and privacy threat based on the ability to permanently save and access information about individuals through temporal and spatial extension of data collection activities. Although concerns about information privacy are not unique to the healthcare domain, health-related information can be perceived as more personal and more sensitive. Due to the highly personal and sensitive nature of healthcare data, both healthcare providers and patients can be expected to resist further digitalization though the usage of RFID technology until security and privacy protections is in place.

There are different kinds of RFID applications that allow healthcare professionals to avoid errors or risks that could endanger the patient safety. Usually, RFID-based sensing activities related to healthcare can be divided in two types:

Direct sensing activity: These activities refer to various identification and monitoring systems. Some of the most promising RFID-based direct sensing activities that have been successfully tested (or deployed) in a number of hospitals include: hospital personnel, patient and newborn identification and monitoring, drug usage monitoring for patients, and smart asset tracking (including surgical instrument tracking and blood bag tracking) [12]. Inevitably, these activities seek to improve patient outcomes and improve the efficiency of the hospital's day-to-day operations.

Indirect inferred activity: These activities basically refer to those systems that use direct sensing activity data to infer important information. For example, detecting pharmaceutical counterfeit, avoiding theft of medical equipment, the tagging of meal plateaux to ensure that patients get proper diet according to their treatment, allergies, and tastes [12].

RFID-based mHealth services have received considerable attention within the healthcare, since early 2007. The technology's promise to efficiently track hospital supplies, medical equipment, medications, and patients is an attractive proposition to the healthcare industry [20]. Some major research challenges related to the development and deployment of RFID-based healthcare are as follows:

RFID tags can be read at a small distance, through materials or clothes. So, the owner of a tag can never be sure when it is being scanned. If the communication between tags and readers is performed in wireless channel, adversary may try to infer personal information to track people remotely. Deployed ubiquitous healthcare systems may have both access permission and privacy invasion problems for the patient's individual medical data that may be overheard by unauthorized persons trying to access the system stealthily.

The information sensed using RFID system may need to be shared with various authorities to access healthcare services. The ID of the tag along with its associated EMR, collected over a period of time, may expose user's private information.

3.2 Privacy Challenges in Cell Phone-Based mHealth Services

In the context of using cell phone-based mHealth services, we generally identify three main security objectives, privacy, integrity, and availability. When considering the perspective of cell phone-based mHealth services, where users typically share personal and medical information in various support groups, preserving privacy is considered to be the most important objective.

The protection of the user's privacy is assumed to be the main objective for cell phone-based mHealth services. Privacy not only encompasses the protection of personal information, which users publish on their profiles, presumably accessible by their contacts only. Privacy is a fundamental human right and personal sensitive information is key factor of privacy. The privacy of sensitive information includes PII (any information that could be used to identify or locate an individual, eg, name, address, or information that can be correlated with other information to identify an individual, eg, credit card number, postal code, etc.). It also includes sensitive information related to religion or race, health, sex, union membership, or other information that is considered private. This information also includes any type of medical condition or medical diagnosis information. When these types of information are stored and processed in the social networking platform, with user-identifiable data contained in the healthcare data, sensitive information about individuals may be easily revealed by analyzing the shared data. Research shows that patient details can be identified through examining identifiers or specific combined demographic data from information (such as age, address, and sex) from each other in certain datasets [7]. Therefore, to provide better privacy facilities to smartphone-based mHealth service users, we need to ensure that sensitive private information is not revealed to any third-party applications.

As part of integrity, the user's identity and data must be protected against unauthorized modification, tampering, and access. In addition to conventional modification detection and message authentication, integrity in the context of social network has to be extended. Parties in a social network structure are not arbitrary devices, but real, unambiguously identifiable persons. The creation of bogus accounts, cloned accounts, or other types of impersonation is easy to achieve in any social network. Identity checks do not necessarily have to be performed by a centralized service; however, all identification services have to be trusted by all participants. In some cases, online social networks might present an option for verifying registered users (in most cases, through email verification processes) in an effort to minimize this problem.

Since some social networks are used as professional tools to aid their members' business or careers, data published by users have to be continuously available. Availability of user profiles is consequently required as a basic feature, even though considering recreational use, the availability of some content may not seem a stringent requirement. In social network, this availability specifically has to include robustness against censorship, and the seizure or hijacking of names and other key words. Apart from availability of data access, availability has to be ensured along with message exchange among members.

3.3 Privacy Challenges in Social Networking and Care Coordination Technologies

Social networking and care coordination technologies allow communities of older adults to connect, share knowledge, and provide support to other older adults and their care providers. These social networks utilize a variety of means to facilitate communication among patients including discussion groups, chat, messaging, email, video, and file sharing. Online social networking and care coordination programs web sites are becoming ever more accessible on mobile devices. For example, care coordination technologies utilize short messaging service or text messages in addition to email notifications for medical appointment reminders, chronic disease management, and health surveys. However, all of these services are prone to user identity leakage. Inevitably, all of these applications are vulnerable to various privacy challenges. The use of data encryption and obfuscation are among a number of approaches to mitigating some of these associated risks.

4. SIGNIFICANCE OF PRIVACY IN mHealth

mHealth applications may have various privacy and security issues. The site may maintain a vast repository of users profile information permanently. Users are increasingly sharing their private details on such sites and, for some people, privacy takes a back seat to the hope that some exchange will help them find a better treatment, manage their condition, or improve overall health. Some people may reveal their health data for the sake of the greater good.

Medical professionals also post sensitive data about their patients, community, and organizations in order to share advice on clinical situations or practice management. Some professionals are even willing to provide personal data in exchange for the utility of the services and the occasional rewards provided by the site. However, once users share their health data with the site, they typically have no control over retention periods for the data or associated metadata that will be maintained in perpetuity. The content produced by users may be revealed to both intended and unintended audiences. Since, anybody can register on the website, anybody can view the content on the site. For example, any person or entity may create fake accounts in order to obtain data from unsuspecting users. Another related issue is that the website may exchange data with third parties without explicit consent. For example, websites like checkMD (http://www.checkMD.com) may disclose users' personal information to its business partners and other third parties. The site may also allows its users to incorporate features created by third parties and let users log into third-party sites using their profile data, which implies that health data available within the protected site might be leaked to the web. Consequently, health data may be exposed to various data recipients without users' knowledge [13].

The accumulated health data can be misused and/or exploited for various nonmedical abuses. Some mHealth applications are commercial companies that have a business model based on harvesting health data for business and proprietary purposes. They may release health data to different data recipients, including doctors, pharmaceutical and medical device companies, researchers, and nonprofit organizations. Aggregated health data are very valuable to commercial companies, such as drug and medical device manufacturers. Innovative data mining and health informatics technologies can link data produced from a variety of different sources to produce useful personal data aggregates or digital dossiers.

Taken in isolation, certain pieces of data do not communicate much about a person, but taken together they could communicate a great deal. The digital dossiers would be immensely valuable to companies looking to market products or, in the case of insurers or employers, deny a policy or a job. The dossiers, when maintained without direct government oversight, could also become an attractive target for hackers and identity thieves. Lastly, another obvious issue is the scale of the security risk. While encrypted transmission will improve confidentiality, and authentication and access control will reduce nonauthorized access, one "hack" into the site, or one error by a site operator, or one misuse by the many other users of the site may compromise the digital profiles of numerous users.

5. SOLVING PRIVACY PROBLEMS WITH VARIOUS METHODS

Due to data privacy, it is essential for users to encrypt their sensitive private data before storing and processing them into the cloud or any other platform. Yet, there exist some shortcomings in the situation of traditional encryption. When a secret key owner wants to look for some data that are stored in the cloud storage, he/she needs to download all the data and decrypt them to perform any type of searching or processing with them. If the encrypted data are huge or the client is a mobile user, then it will be very inefficient and is not feasible. Otherwise he/she must send a key to the server that is, in turn, used to perform the decryption and search procedures. In *"Provable Data Possession"* model ensures the possession of data files on untrusted storages. It uses a Rivest–Shamir–Adleman homomorphic linear authenticator for auditing outsourced data, but this model leaks the data to external auditors and hence, is not provably privacy-preserving. Juels *et al.* [14] describe a *"Proof of Retrievability"* model, where spot-checking and error-correcting codes are used in order to ensure possession and retrievability. This scheme only works for encrypted files that requires the auditor to keep state and suffers from bounded usage, which potentially adds online burden to users when the keyed hashes are used up.

In the following section, we briefly describe some existing methodologies that guarantee privacy.

5.1 Encryption Methods

There are a number of approaches that make use of encryption techniques to achieve privacy in the cloud. Wessel [12] proposed the design of privacy-preserving cloud storage framework to solve privacy security problem, this comprises the design of data organization structure, the generation and management of keys, the interaction between participants and the handling of change of user's access right and also supports the dynamic operations of data. It uses an interactive protocol and an extirpation-based key derivation algorithm. A method for improving user privacy with secret key recovery in cloud storage that allows users' to encrypt their files in the cloud storage has been proposed in Ref. [11]. Here, a Secret sharing Algorithm to Key Recovery Mechanism is used. In this technique, the user's privacy is protected and it decreases the risk of encryption key lose. But it puts a big computation burden for users. It has concerns about transforming speed. Renewing user's key is a challenge here, users cannot search words and there is dispersal of information. Wessel [12] provides a privacy-preserving cloud storage framework supporting *ciphertext* retrieval. This is used to preserve the privacy of data through encryption while reducing the data owner's workload pertaining to the management and sharing of data. Interaction protocol, Key Derivation Algorithm, a combination of Symmetric and Asymmetric encryption, and Bloom Filter are all useful privacy-preservation methods. They can operate on encrypted data; reduce data owner's workload on managing the data and storage space; reduce communication, computation, and storage overhead. It can manage numerous keys and is efficient, safe, and economic. But it supports only owner-write-user-read and lacks in technique that support ciphertext-based computing. The main problem in using encryption-based technique is that it limits the data usage and puts into an additional burden. The access control mechanisms are available which will overcome the burden of the earlier overheads.

5.2 Access Control Mechanisms

Access control mechanisms that provide privacy have been discussed at length (http://www.checkMD.com) [8]. Pearson discussed a privacy-preserving access control scheme for securing data in clouds that verifies the authenticity of the user without knowing the user's identity before storing information [8]. Here only valid users are able to decrypt the stored information. It prevents reply attack, achieves authenticity, and privacy. It is decentralized and robust which allows multiple read and write, distributed access control and the identity of user is protected. In the access policy for each record stored in the cloud should be known and should be based on the assumption that cloud administrators are honest though it does not support complex access controls (http://www.checkMD.com).

5.3 Remote Data Checking Using Provable Data Possession

Ateniese *et al.* [15] introduce a model for provable data possession that can be used for remote data checking. By having a sampling random set of blocks from the server, this model produces probabilistic proofs of possession that will significantly reduce input/output costs. In order to minimize network communication, the challenge/response protocol transmits a small and constant amount of data. The model incorporates some mechanisms for mitigating arbitrary amounts of data corruption and it is robust. It offers two efficient secure packet data protocol (PDP) schemes and the overhead at the server is low. To add robustness to any remote data checking scheme based on spot-checking it proposes a generic transformation.

5.4 Privacy-Preserving Data Integrity Checking

A privacy-preserving remote data integrity checking protocol with data dynamics and public verifiability [16] makes use of a Remote Data Integrity Checking Protocol. The protocol provides public verifiability without the help of a third-party auditor. It does not leak any privacy information to third-party, which provides good performance without the support of the trusted third-party and provides a method for independent arbitration of data retention contracts. But it gives unnecessary computation and communication cost.

5.5 Privacy-Preserving Public Auditability

Some recent studies have examined problems with ensuring the integrity of data storage in cloud computing [8]. It allows a third-party auditor to confirm the integrity of dynamic data stored in the cloud. This scheme achieves both public auditability and dynamic data operations. The authors in Ref. [17] propose the use of a privacy-preserving public auditor for secure cloud storage. The protocol design necessary to achieve optimal security and performance guarantees like: Public Auditability, Storage Correctness,

Privacy-Preserving, Batch auditing, and to be Lightweight. It relies on third-party auditors and has the use of expensive modular exponentiation operations that leads to storage overhead on server and extra communication cost. Gellman [17] proposes an efficient audit service outsourcing for data integrity in clouds. It is based upon the creation of an interactive PDP to inhibit the leakage of verified data. It describes the periodic verification for improving the performance of audit services. Here, the approach adopts a way of sampling verification. The scheme not only prevents the deception and forgery of cloud storage providers but also prevents the leakage of outsourced data in the process of verification. It supports an adaptive parameter selection. The system shows only lower computation cost as well as a shorter extra storage and the scheme is less complex due to fragment structure. It achieves Audit-without-downloading, Verification-correctness, Privacy-preservation, and High-performance.

6. CONCLUSION

The rapid evolution of mobile technology coupled with the rapid growth of various forms of mHealth poses both challenges and opportunities for the adoption and diffusion of mHealth. There are a number of issues that are particularly pertinent to how mHealth will be deployed in the coming years, and how rapidly it will become an integral part of the healthcare system. However, to ensure widespread adoption of mHealth-based services at all level of society, we need to address the privacy challenges posed by the underlying technology.

REFERENCES

[1] S. Adibi, Link technologies and BlackBerry mobile health (mHealth) solutions: a review, IEEE Trans. Inf. Technol. Biomed. 14 (4) (2012) 586–597.
[2] S. Adibi, Biomedical sensing analyzer (BSA) for Mobile-Health (mHealth)-LTE, in: Special Issue on Emerging Technologies in Communications—mHealth (Healthcare Based on Mobile Phone Technology), IEEE Journal on Selected Areas in Communications (JSAC)—Area 1: e-Health, paper #: 1569578555, March 2012.
[3] HIPAA-General Information. http://www.cms.gov/HIPAAGenInfo/.
[4] B.C.M. Fung, K. Wang, R. Chen, P.S. Yu, Privacy-preserving data publishing: a survey on recent developments, ACM Comput. Surv. 42 (4) (2010) 1–53.
[5] C.C. Aggarwal, P.S. Yu, A general survey of privacy-preserving data mining models and algorithms, in: The Kluwer International Series on Advances in Database Systems, vol. 34, Springer, USA, 2008, pp. 11–52.
[6] E. Harry, A. Smith, Context-Based Access Control Model for HIPAA Privacy and Security Compliance, SANS Institute, USA, 2001.

[7] R. Lillian, Y. Nytr, Personalized access control for a personally controlled health record, in: Proceedings of the 2nd ACM Workshop on Computer Security Architectures, Alexandria, Virginia, USA, 2008, pp. 9–16.

[8] S. Pearson, Taking account of privacy when designing cloud computing services, in: Proceeding of ICSE-Cloud 09, Vancouver, 2009.

[9] C. Wang, Q. Wang, K. Ren, W. Lou, Privacy-preserving public auditing for data storage security in cloud computing, in: Proceedings of INFOCOM'10, 2010, pp. 1–9.

[10] W. Itani, A. Kayssi, A. Chehab, Privacy as a service: privacy-aware data storage and processing in cloud computing architectures, in: Proceeding of DASC'09, 2009, pp. 711–716.

[11] R.L. Juban, D.C. Wyld, Would you like chips with that? Consumer perspectives of RFID, Manage. Res. News 27 (11) (2004) 29–44.

[12] R. Wessel, RFID bands at the Jacobi Medical Center, 2005). Last accessed—March 2012 at, http://www.rfidgazette.org/2005/12/rfid_bands_at_t.html.

[13] F. Rahman, I.D. Addo, S.I. Ahamed, PriSN: a privacy protection framework for healthcare social networking sites, in: Proceedings of the 2014 Conference on Research in Adaptive and Convergent Systems, 2014, pp. 66–71.

[14] K.D. Bowers, A. Juels, A. Oprea, Proofs of retrievability: theory and implementation, in: Proceedings of the 2009 ACM Workshop on Cloud Computing Security (CCSW'09), 2009.

[15] G. Ateniese, R. Burns, R. Curtmola, J. Herring, O. Khan, L. Kissner, Z. Peterson, D. Song, Remote data checking using provable data possession, ACM Trans. Inf. Syst. Secur. 14 (1) (2011) 12.

[16] J.-J. Yang, J. Li, N. Yu, A hybrid solution for medical data sharing in the cloud environment, Futur. Gener. Comput. Syst. 43–44 (2015) 74–86.

[17] R. Gellman, WPF REPORT: Privacy in the Clouds: Risks to Privacy and Confidentiality from Cloud Computing, 23 February 2009.

[18] J. Li, J.-J. Yang, C. Liu, B. Liu, Z. Yu, Y. Shi, Exploiting semantic linkages among multiple sources for semantic information retrieval, Enterp. Inf. Syst. 8 (4) (2014) 464–489.

[19] J.Q. Li, J.-J. Yang, Y. Zhao, B. Liu, A topdown approach for approximate data anonymisation, Enterp. Inf. Syst. 7 (3) (2013) 272–302.

[20] J.-J. Yang, J. Li, J. Mulder, et al., Emerging information technologies for enhanced healthcare. Comput. Ind. 69 (2015) 3–11, http://dx.doi.org/10.1016/j.compind. 2015.01.012.

ABOUT THE AUTHORS

Farzana Rahman, PhD, is an Assistant Professor (Computer Science) at James Madison University, USA. She is also a member of ACM and IEEE. Farzana's scholarly interests include information security, mobile computing, pervasive systems, mHealth, computer science education, outreach programs, technology and gender, and technology for development. Farzana has a number of published peer-reviewed conference papers.

Ivor D. Addo is an Adjunct Assistant Professor (IT/Management) and a PhD candidate at Marquette University, USA. He is also a member of ACM and IEEE. Ivor's research interests are focused on privacy and security issues in IoT and Sociable Robotic applications. Ivor has a number of published peer-reviewed conference papers.

Sheikh Iqbal Ahamed is a Professor and Director of the Ubicomp Lab in the Department of Mathematics, Statistics, and Computer Science at Marquette University, USA. He is also a faculty member of Medical College of Wisconsin, USA. He is a senior member of the IEEE Computer Society and ACM. He completed his PhD in Computer Science from Arizona State University,

USA in 2003. His research interests include mHealth, security, and privacy in pervasive computing and middleware for ubiquitous/pervasive computing. He has published 100+ peer-reviewed journal, conference, and workshop papers including nine best paper/posters. Dr. Ahamed serves regularly on international conference program committees in software engineering and pervasive computing such as COMPSAC 13, COMPSAC 12, PERCOM 08, and SAC 08. He is the Guest Editor of *Computer Communications Journal*, Elsevier.

Dr. Ji-jiang Yang is a Professor at Tsinghua University in Beijing, China. His research interests include mHealth/eHealth, security and privacy, and big data. He currently has a number of research grants in the eHealth/mHealth area. He has a number of collaborative healthcare projects with researchers from different universities and nonprofit organizations in China. He has published 100+ peer-reviewed journal, conference, and workshop papers. Dr. Yang serves regularly on international conference program committees in medical data analysis and applications such as MEDICOMP and COMPSAC. He is currently the Workshops Chair for COMPSAC 2017. He is also a Guest Editor of a couple of special issues.

Dr. Qing Wang is a Research Scientist at Tsinghua University in Beijing, China. His research interests include computer security and reliability, computer communications (networks), and information systems (business informatics). He continues to work on a number of healthcare projects. Dr. Wang has published 20+ peer-reviewed journal, conference, and workshop papers.

CHAPTER THREE

A Survey of Data Cleansing Techniques for Cyber-Physical Critical Infrastructure Systems

M. Woodard, M. Wisely, S. Sedigh Sarvestani
Missouri University of Science and Technology, Rolla, MO, United States

Contents

Advances in Computers, Volume 102
ISSN 0065-2458
http://dx.doi.org/10.1016/bs.adcom.2016.05.002

Abstract

Critical infrastructure cyber-physical systems heavily depend on accurate data in order to facilitate intelligent control and improve performance. Corruption of data in these systems is unavoidable, resulting from both intentional and unintentional means. The consequence of making control decisions based on erroneous or corrupted data can be severe including financial loss, injury, or death. This makes employing a mechanism to detect and mitigate corrupted data crucial. Many techniques have been developed to detect and mitigate corrupted data. However, these techniques vary greatly in their capability to detect certain anomalies and required computing resources. This chapter presents a survey of data cleansing techniques and their applicability to various control levels in a critical infrastructure cyber-physical systems.

1. INTRODUCTION

Modern society is becoming more and more dependent on access to accurate real-time and stored information. Critical infrastructure systems are not different as they transition from purely physical systems to critical infrastructure cyber-physical systems (CPSs) to meet performance requirements and growing demands. In a CPS, a layer of cyber infrastructure is added to the physical infrastructure to improve functionality. This cyber infrastructure consists of intelligent embedded systems, communication capabilities, distributed computing, and intelligent control [1]. The cyber infrastructures facilitate intelligent control to better adapt to changes in demand and production. Smart power grids, intelligent water distribution networks, and smart transportation systems are all examples of modern CPSs.

Intelligent control systems in CPSs make decisions by processing real-time and previously stored data. The intelligent control systems calculate optimal control settings by processing data from the controllers immediate area as well as system-wide data. Processing data from system-wide sources prevents adverse consequences caused by localized control. Bakken *et al.* [2] discuss how the use of real-time measurements can address many of the power generation and distribution challenges in the smart grid. Hoverstad *et al.* [3] discuss the need for data cleansing on load prediction algorithms used in the smart grid. Specifically the added robustness achieved by removing sensor data errors prior to executing the prediction algorithms.

CPS reliance on real-time field data makes the systems susceptible to severe consequences caused by corrupted data. Buttyán et al. [4] presents the design and protection challenges of cyber infrastructure in CPSs, discussing fault tolerance, security, and privacy of sensor nodes, networking protocols, and operating systems. One example of severe consequences resulting from cyber infrastructure failure in a stock market is discussed by Kirilenko et al. [5]. In Aug. 2012, a financial computing system failure consisting of a software error cost the mid-size financial firm Knight Capital $10 million per minute. While this failure had economic consequences, failures in other critical infrastructure and manufacturing systems could result in physical injury or loss of life. To prevent these failures it is essential to detect and mitigate data failures. This process is known as data cleansing.

The motivation for the survey presented in this chapter are the catastrophic critical infrastructure failures in recent history. Miller et al. [6] discuss the failure of a Bellingham, WA gas pipeline which ruptured and within 1 1/2 h leaked 237,000 gallons of gasoline into a creek flowing through Whatcom Falls Park in Jun. 1999. The gasoline ignited burning approximately 1 1/2 mi of forest along the creek killing three people and injuring eight others. Due to the company's practice of performing live database development work on critical components, real-time sensor data was unavailable to control systems. As a result, the control systems were unable to react to the failure. Another failure, discussed by Berizzi [7] and Buldyrev et al. [8], occurred in Italy on Sept. 28, 2003. The failure was triggered by a single-line failure near the Swiss–Italian border, which caused a cascading failure resulting in half of Italy being without power for multiple days. This local failure led to Internet communication network nodes failures, which in turn caused further breakdown of the power systems control. Although these examples are not the result of corrupted data, they demonstrate how CPSs rely on accurate, real-time data and the potential for failures induced by data corruption.

This chapter serves as an extension to our previous work [9], presents a survey of data cleansing techniques, and classifies them based on their applicability in CPSs. Fig. 1 is a taxonomy of the topics presented in this chapter drawing from recent papers as shown in Fig. 2.

The remainder of this chapter is structured as follows. In Section 2, we introduce an example Intelligent Transportation System, which is a type of CPSs. This example application will be used for comparison of techniques. In Section 3, we discuss sources of corrupted data and introduce a number of data cleansing techniques. In Section 4, we classify techniques based on the

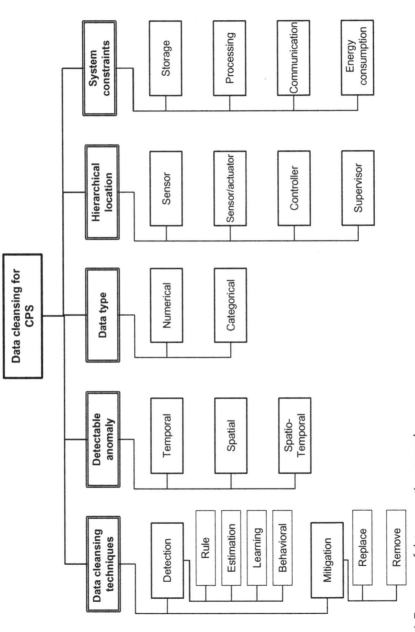

Fig. 1 Taxonomy of data corruption research.

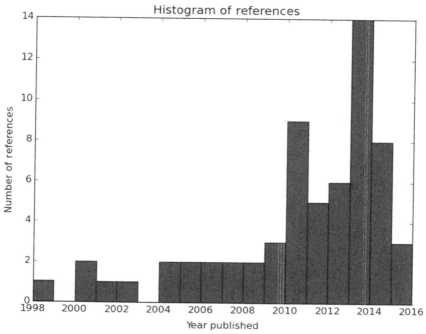

Fig. 2 Histogram of papers cited.

type of anomalies which can be detected and mitigated. In Section 5, we classify techniques based on hardware, communication and time constraints. In Section 6, we classify techniques based on the type of data which can be cleansed by each technique. In Section 7, we classify techniques based on their hierarchical location within the system. Lastly, Section 8 addresses future directions for this research.

2. RUNNING ITS EXAMPLE

Intelligent Transportation Systems (ITSs) are CPSs aimed at improving performance and safety of transportation networks [10]. ITS refers to all modes of transport including road, rail and air. All of these transportation systems have similar challenges [11]. However, road transportation systems are used as an example system in this chapter. All following references to ITS will refer to road transportation systems.

ITS technologies include everything from basic traffic management systems such as vehicle navigation and traffic signal control to more advanced systems that allow vehicle to everything (V2X) communication to improve control and information dissemination between vehicles, roadside units, infrastructure, pedestrians, and cyclists [12]. ITS technologies also include unmanned vehicle technologies including self-driving vehicles and automatic parking systems. The example ITS system used in this chapter focuses on infrastructure to vehicle (I2V), vehicle to vehicle (V2V), and vehicle to infrastructure (V2I) communication as well as information dissemination and the intelligent traffic control that communication facilitates [13].

Fig. 3 depicts the cyber and physical layers of an example ITS.

These services can be classified based on where in the infrastructure the required computer processing occurs. Elements of ITS infrastructure can be classified as mobile infrastructure or static infrastructure.

2.1 Mobile Infrastructure

Mobile infrastructure consists of all ITS elements without a static network connection, ie, vehicles.

Vehicles on modern roadways range from classic cars with no digital systems to fully autonomous, unmanned vehicles. ITS systems must be designed to accommodate the full range of vehicles. We will categorize vehicles into three classes based on their functionality: traditional, intelligent and unmanned vehicles.

Traditional vehicles are all vehicles without V2V or V2I communication capability. They do not provide data directly to the ITS. Vehicles in this category may or may not have I2V capabilities which would provide the driver with additional information about congestion, such as two-way GPS traffic updates. This category also includes vehicles with adaptive cruises control or advanced collision avoidance systems such as blind spot sensors and backup sensors. While these technologies improve vehicle safety and control, they do not provide data to other components in an ITS.

Intelligent vehicles are vehicles with V2V or V2I communication capability that are controlled by a human driver. These vehicles are equipped with an on-board sensor suite with the capability to monitor the locations and actions of surrounding vehicles as well as detect road obstacles and conditions. These vehicles utilize on-board processing and storage systems to analyze collected data. Collected information is communicated to surrounding vehicles or the ITS infrastructure via roadside unit (RSU). The wireless communications capability falls into two categories based on the indented recipient. Short-range communication is used to communicate with neighboring vehicles and RSUs using the IEEE 802.11p protocol, which was

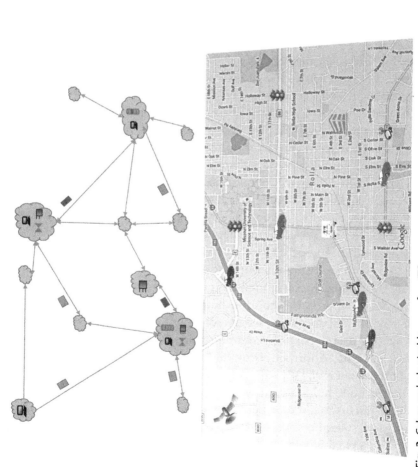

Fig. 3 Cyber and physical layers of an ITS.

Cyber connection

Traffic sensor

Smart traffic light

Connected vehicle

Nonconnected vehicle

Central traffic management

GPS

Cyber layer

Controller

Database

Sensor

Processing

Corrupted data packet

Correct data packet

specifically developed for ITS and mobile ad hoc or mesh networking. The second type of communication is longer range communications using IEEE 802.16, WiMAX, GSM, or 3G. This type of communication is used to communicate with a central traffic management center or to access other relevant data sources.

Unmanned vehicles are vehicles with the same capabilities as intelligent vehicles. However, the collected data is used to directly control the vehicle rather than to assist a human driver. In addition, collected data may be provided to other components of an ITS.

2.2 Static Infrastructure

Static infrastructure within ITS includes purely physical infrastructure including roads, highways, and bridges as well as the static, cyber-enhanced infrastructure. The static ITS infrastructure does not move during operation and includes devices such as traffic signals and road sensors.

The cyber layer of an ITS system is structured and functions similar to a sensor database architecture. Sensor database architectures are classified based on where the data is stored. These architectures range from traditional sensor databases, where the data is stored in a centralized database, to distributed databases, where every sensor node has its own database.

Traditional sensor networks described by Akyildiz et al. [14] are not applicable to ITS due to large networking overhead and delay. Another sensor network architecture is the distributed sensor database system, which places databases closer to the controller and sensor nodes. This architecture can be thought of as a data logging network. In this type of sensor network, all sensors send all sensed data to secondary storage, which can be retrieved in bulk. This architecture permits duplication of stored data to improve performance. Distributed database architectures are not specific to sensor networks. Many approaches to distributed databases are summarized by Hurson et al. [15] including federated and multidatabases which address issues such as data distribution and transparency as well as query and transaction processing. A further distributed sensor network architecture is discussed by Bonnet et al. [16] is the sensor database model. In this architecture, each sensor node holds a database that can be dynamically queried. Tsiftes et al. [17] discuss this sensor network architecture and propose a database management system.

A practical ITS would use a combination of distributed and sensor database architectures at various hierarchical levels of the system. Combining these architectures may improve performance by limiting the communication of raw data, energy, bandwidth, and scalability. Additionally, this architecture improves maintainability and fault recovery by storing performance data at the sensor nodes. Amadeo *et al.* [12] discuss the benefits of using a Named Data Networking model for ITS. Which would require this type of database architecture. However, this architecture has challenges including the system updates and database management due to its distributed nature.

2.2.1 Roadside Units

A roadside unit (RSU) collects traffic data from a static sensing area along a road and transmits data to traffic control devices as well as a central traffic management center. These devices also serve as an information source for intelligent vehicles to collect future traffic information [18].

RSU can sense traffic information using a number of methods. One method for collecting traffic information is the triangulation method. Triangulation uses mobile phones as anonymous traffic probes. The phones transmit presence announcement signals to the mobile phone network which can be observed by an RSU. This network data is collected and analyzed using triangulation and converted into traffic flow information. This method works for all types of vehicles, provided that a powered-on mobile phone is in the vehicle. Another method is vehicle reidentification. This method uses some unique identification from an in-vehicle devices, such as Bluetooth MAC addresses or an RFID toll tags. As a vehicle travels along a route, multiple RSUs detect a specific vehicle and record a time stamp. This information is shared and analyzed to determine speed, travel times, and traffic flow for a road segment. This method requires technology within the vehicle to transmit a unique id. Conveniently, most modern vehicles use wireless communication between components, which can be used to identify a vehicle. Lastly, V2I communication provided by intelligent vehicles can be used to collect traffic flow data. Many other techniques can be used to collect traffic flow data such as two-way GPS or satellite navigation systems, inductive loop detection, traffic video cameras, and audio detection.

RSUs use information from multiple sources to create an accurate picture of traffic flow on a specific road segment by using data fusion-based approaches to intelligently combine data. These data fusion techniques create a more accurate representation of the traffic than any single sensing method.

2.2.2 Traffic Control

ITS allows for traffic control systems that are more advanced than traditional timed traffic signals [19]. One type of control device is intelligent traffic lights, which use traffic data collected at the local intersection, as well as future traffic information provided by RSUs, to create a dynamic time schedule to maximize the flow of traffic through an intersection. Another control system is variable speed limits. These systems work to minimize traffic density in congested areas by dynamically changing the speed limit of roads based on weather conditions, road conditions, or the presence of congestion areas. Lastly, dynamic lanes can be used to provide more inbound or outbound lanes depending on the flow of traffic as traffic in many metropolitan areas is not symmetric.

2.2.3 Central Traffic Management

A central traffic management (CTM) system could be centralized or distributed over a control area. In either case, a CTM collects and analyzes data from intelligent vehicles, unmanned vehicles, and RSU to facilitate control decisions [20]. Each central traffic management office would have a server for data storage and processing. The processed data could be used for high-level coordination of the traffic control devices. The central office could then broadcast data back to vehicles to improve navigation and control.

3. DATA CLEANSING TECHNIQUES

In general, data cleansing involves exploring a data set, detecting possible problems, and attempting to correct detected errors [21]. Definitions of data cleansing vary depending on the field and application.

Traditionally, data cleansing was the detection and removal of duplicated records of differing formats. This type of data cleansing was conducted in data warehouses and executed when multiple databases are merged, also called merge and purge [22]. Duplicate identification in warehouse data cleansing is also called record linkage, semantic integration, instance identification, or object identity problem. Bertossi et al. [23] discuss matching dependencies for data cleaning of similar attributes for clean query answering. Modern cleansing also includes detection of erroneous data. This type of data cleansing is a part of data/information quality management referred to as Total Quality Data Management (TQDM) [24]. In line with TQDM, Dallachiesa et al. [25] present NADEEF as an end-to-end off-the-shelf semiautomatic data cleansing solution. Budka *et al.* [26] present the challenges of data preprocessing and cleansing for prediction in control systems using soft sensors identifying some if the key challenges. This type of data cleansing is directly applicable to critical infrastructure CPS applications, in which a huge amount of data is collected and used for control. TQDM includes clerical error and organizational behavior aspects which are beyond the scope of CPS applications.

Data cleansing, as it pertains to CPSs, occurs in two phases: detection and mitigation, as described in Woodard *et al.* [9]. Before we discuss detection and mitigation techniques, an overview of the sources of erroneous data is presented.

3.1 Sources Data Errors

In order to discuss sources of erroneous data, an overview of fault tolerance and dependability terminology is necessary. More detailed discussions are provided in Aviźienis *et al.* [27]. In fault tolerance and dependability, a system is described as being in a specific state in the presence of a disruptive event based on the systems ability to provide its specified service. The terms used to describe the threats to system operation are failure, error, and fault. A system failure is the state in which a system does not comply with system specifications. An error is a system state that may induce a failure. More specifically, a failure occurs when an error causes an alteration of the system services. A fault is the cause of an error. Faults are classified based on their persistence, activity, and intent. Corrupted or erroneous data can be a failure, an error, or a fault depending on its location in the system. Producing corrupted data is a system failure; processing corrupted data is a system error; accepting corrupted data as input is a system fault. Erroneous data can be created within a system via intentional and unintentional means.

Intentionally erroneous data is the result of an attack. Attacks can be classified as purely cyber, purely physical, or combined cyber-physical depending on the source of the attack. Mo *et al.* [28] describe these types of attacks on critical infrastructure systems. An example of a cyber-physical attack on an intelligent water distribution system is provided by Amin *et al.* [29].

Unintentionally erroneous data is the result of corruption during communication, processing, or storage in addition to inaccurate sensor readings. Cebula *et al.* [30] provide a very detailed taxonomy of cyber and physical risks to computer communication, processing, or storage information

technology assets. The input data to a system may be erroneous as Aggarwal
et al. [31] discuss the need for data cleaning of sensor readings. Sensor readings are often created by the inherently noisy process of converting a measured quantity such as voltage into another measured quantities such as
temperature. Additionally, errors can be introduced by external conditions,
sensor aging, miscalibration, or intermittent failures of sensors. However, in
many large distributed systems, the cause of the erroneous data is difficult to
determine and the same data cleansing techniques may be used regardless of
the source of the data error.

3.2 Data Error Detection

As stated above, data errors can be produced by a number of sources including miscalibrated or faulty sensor hardware as well as errors in processing,
storage, and communication. The detection phase of data cleansing is the
identification of potential errors. In general, this is done by locating anomalies in the system. Rajasegarar *et al.* [32] discuss the importance and general
challenges of anomaly detection in sensor networks as it pertains to fault
diagnosis, intrusion detection, and monitoring applications. The primary
challenge in the development of any anomaly detection algorithm is that
sensor networks are highly application and domain dependent. Examples
of domain specific techniques are proposed by Yin *et al.* [33], who model
wind turbine data, and Freeman *et al.* [34], who model aircraft pilot-static
probe data. Both of these anomaly detection techniques are able to detect
anomalies in data with significant measurement noise and unknown distribution. However, these techniques are not suitable for other domains and do
not scale to the size of CPSs. Another major issue in CPS data corruption
detection is determining when anomalous data is truly a data error. Tang
et al. [35] investigate the trustworthiness of sensor data and propose a method
called Tru-Alarm to eliminate false alarms by filtering out noise and false
information. Tru-Alarm is able to estimate the source of an alarm by con-
structing an alarm graph and conducting trustworthiness inference based on
the graph links.

Detection techniques can be classified by the method employed to
detect potential data errors. Zhang *et al.* [36], Chandola *et al.* [37], and Fang
et al. [38] provide comprehensive overviews of anomaly detection techniques. Table 1 is a summary of these approaches and recent advances
in anomaly detection. These approaches include statistical detection and
behavioral detection approaches. Statistical detection approaches can be

Table 1 Summary of Statistical Anomaly Detection Approaches

Detection Approaches	Description
Rule based	Rule-based detection approaches set acceptable limits for data values. These limits can be determined from an outlier set or using statistical inference.
Estimation based	Estimation-based detection approaches use probability distribution models of the data to detect anomalous values. These approaches require knowledge of the data distribution or the use of histograms or kernel density estimators to assume a distribution. They are mathematically proven to detect anomalies if the correct distribution model is used.
Learning based	Learning-based detection approaches utilize data mining, clustering, and classification algorithms to group data. Anomalies are detected when the new data does not belong to a group.
Behavior based	Behavior-based detection approaches utilize signature, anomaly, and stateful protocol analysis of a system to detect anomalies in system behavior.

further classified into estimation-based, rule-based, and learning-based detection and hybrid approaches.

3.3 Statistical Detection

Data errors can be detected by locating data anomalies or statistical irregularities in the data. Faulty sensors typically report easily distinguishable extreme or unrealistic values, however, not all data anomalies are the result of erroneous data. Extreme environmental variations can produce data anomalies that should be distinguished from data errors. Statistical anomaly detection approaches detect anomalies by checking how well the data fits a statistical distribution model of the data. Anomalies are detected when data values fall outside an acceptable tolerance set by the user. Statistical anomaly detection uses statistical metrics such as mean, standard deviation, and range. to estimate normal data values and detects outliers if the data falls outside this expected range. The statistical model used to capture the distribution of the data can be assumed or estimated based on previously recorded data.

3.3.1 Estimation-Based Detection

Estimation-based statistical approaches use probability distribution models of the data to detect anomalous values. Probability distribution models can be parametric or nonparametric based [36]. Parametric models assume knowledge of the data distribution, ie, Gaussian-based model. Nonparametric models such as histograms and kernel density estimators, do not assume knowledge of the data distribution. Histogram models estimate the probability of data occurrences by counting the frequency of occurrence and detect anomalies by comparing the new data with each of the categories in the histogram. Kernel density estimators estimate the probability distribution function (pdf) for some normal data. An anomaly is detected if new data lies in the low probability region of the pdf. Fang *et al.* [39] propose an energy efficient detection method using an ARIMA model. The ARIMA model is a statistical model used in time series analysis. It has three terms, autoregression (AR), integration (I), and moving average (MA) to represent the data. The autoregression term compares the new value to historical data using linear regression. The integration term differences the original data series to make the process stationary. The moving average term captures the influence of extreme values. Each sensor node maintains a matrix of all maximum and minimum differences between itself and its neighbors. Then, using a voting mechanism, values are marked as valid or erroneous. Some estimation-based statistical approaches do, however, have the potential to bias the cleansed data. Bilir *et al.* [40] show that an incorrectly computed residual covariance matrix while using sparse inverse covariance estimation method can result in data errors. The miscalculation can lead to the sequential removal of good data eventually leading to a biased estimation. The authors also present a method to correct this error.

Estimation-based approaches are mathematically proven to detect anomalies if a correct probability distribution model is used. However, knowledge of the probability distribution is unavailable in many real-world applications, making nonparametric approaches more useful. Nonparametric approaches require additional hardware and storage, but they are able to detect anomalies very quickly.

3.3.2 Rule-Based Detection

Rule-based statistical approaches are the simplest form of anomaly detection. An acceptable lower and upper limit for the data is set and any value outside of this range is an anomaly. This technique requires only the definition of an outlier to be set, making it inflexible and resulting in many false positives or undetected anomalies if the tolerance is set too low or high. The benefits of this technique are that it is fast, requires no additional storage capability, and can be implemented in few lines of code, making it ideal for sensor nodes.

Another simple rule-based statistical approach to anomaly detection is statistical inference using the mean and variance of a data set. Ngai *et al.* [41] use a chi-square test performed over a sliding window. In this example, the system determines that at least one value in the sliding window is anomalous if the chi-square value falls outside of a range specified by the user. The acceptable level must be configured prior to operation. This node-local approach can detect anomalies in the data stream of a single sensor while imposing no additional network overhead. Statistical inference techniques cannot adapt to changing ranges, which are very common in long-term wireless sensor network installations. Panda *et al.* [42] propose another very simple rule-based anomaly detection method which calculates the mean and variance of a set of neighboring sensors to determine if a sensor is faulty. Rule-based statistical methods can be implemented on minimal hardware and detect anomalies very quickly provided the data is well behaved and the rules are set appropriately. As such, other approaches have been developed that do not rely on user-set parameters.

3.3.3 Learning-Based Detection

Learning-based statistical approaches utilize data mining, clustering, and classification algorithms to group data based on data similarities [38]. An anomaly is detected when the data does not belong to a group. These techniques have very high detection rates but require additional processing and storage hardware.

A decentralized clustering approach to anomaly detection is set forth by Rajasegarar *et al.* [43]. This approach was designed specifically for hierarchical (tree-based) networks. Leaf nodes take sensor readings and cluster them into fixed-width clusters. Each nonleaf node in the tree takes clusters from its children and merges them together. Anomaly detection is performed at the root node by finding clusters that are further away from other clusters by more than one standard deviation above the average cluster distance. Chang *et al.* [44] use an echo state network (ESN), a neural network in which all neurons are connected to each other, to perform anomaly detection. The ESNs are trained before the nodes are deployed, so they are not very flexible. They operate in a similar fashion to Bayesian networks where the sensor's value is compared to the value predicted by the ESN. The advantage of using a neural net in this case is that it has much lower CPU and RAM requirements than a Bayesian network. An improvement to this approach is put forth by Obst [45]. Instead of building recurrent neural networks beforehand, each node communicates with its immediate neighbors to build a model of the values observed by its sensors. This model is then used to estimate anomalies in the readings.

Classification approaches use a learned model to organize data into classes; in this case, normal or anomalous. One classification approach uses Bayesian networks to model sensor values and predict when values are anomalous [38]. Mayfield et al. [46] have developed a tool called ERACER that uses relational dependency networks to correct anomalous data and fill in missing data. The tool runs on a sensor network base station and develops linear models of sensor data, taking into account readings from other sensors at that node and readings from neighbor nodes. Another example using Bayesian networks is Ref. [47], where the concentration of various gases in a mine's atmosphere is monitored. The network models sensor values over time as well as physical relationships between sensors. The system learns a baseline for the mine's gas concentrations that adapts to the natural fluctuations in gas concentration. It can detect both single-sensor anomalies and multinode anomalies and events.

Ni et al. [48] propose using a hierarchical Bayesian space–time model to detect trustworthy sensors. The disadvantage of this technique is the amount of work required to set up the model. This technique results in excellent anomaly detection if the model accurately represents the data. However, as with all models, if the model is poorly matched to the data, the system performance degrades. A more advanced classification approach is the nearest neighbor approach. This approach uses a distance metric, for example Euclidean distance, to determine how similar a value is to its neighbors. An anomaly is detected if the distance between neighbors is more than a user-specified threshold. Expanding on this approach, Branch et al. [49] use a distributed algorithm to detect outliers as the data propagates through a sensor network. In this approach, each node maintains a set of outlier data points from itself and its neighbors. A ranking function is used to map data values to nonnegative real numbers which indicate the degree to which the data value can be regarded as an outlier with respect to the data set. Nodes transmit data they suspect will cause the outlier set of their neighbors to change. This is similar to a distributed k-nearest-neighbors classification approach. This technique is flexible with respect to the outlier definition, allowing for dynamic updating and in-network detection, reducing bandwidth and energy consumption.

A method to improve the performance of learning-based approaches uses principal component analysis (PCA) to reduce the dimensionality of a data. PCA is a technique that uses spectral decomposition to find normal behavior in a data set. PCA is used to reduce dimensionality before detection by finding a subset of data which captures the behavior of the data. Chitradevi *et al.* [50] propose a two-step algorithm. First, a PCA model is built that can be used for fault detection. Second, the mahalanobis distance is used to determine the similarity between the current sensor readings against the developed sensor data model. However, conventional PCA approaches are sensitive to data anomaly frequency in collected data and fail to detect slow and long-duration anomalies. Xie *et al.* [51] address this problem by using a multiscale principal component analysis (MSPCA) to detect anomalies and extract and interpret information. MSPCA uses both wavelet analysis and principal component analysis. The time–frequency information of the data is captured using wavelet analysis while principal component analysis is used to detect data anomalies. This technique allows for detecting gradual and persistent anomalies with different time–frequency features.

3.3.4 Hybrid Detection

Lastly, a hybrid approach is proposed by Warriach *et al.* [52] to detect data anomalies based on the three methods. Combining rule-based methods, estimation-based, and learning-based methods, they are able to leverage domain and expert knowledge, sensor spatial and temporal correlations and inferred models for the faulty sensor readings using training data. This approach has the benefits of the above approaches and also requires more processing capability and power at sensor nodes.

3.4 Behavioral Detection

Behavioral detection approaches have also been implemented to detect the erroneous data in the system by detecting anomalous behavior of a system rather than analysis of the data. Many of these approaches were developed as a part of intrusion detection systems (IDS). Liao *et al.* [53] provide a comprehensive overview and classification of general computing IDS approaches. These classifications are signature-based detection, anomaly-based detection, and stateful protocol analysis. Signature-based detection, also known as knowledge-based detection, detects a pattern or a string that corresponds to a known attack. This technique is limited to detecting known attacks from previously analyzed events. Anomaly-based detection determines the normal behavior of the system and detects anomalies by comparing the current behavior with the normal behavior model. Anomaly-based detection can monitor any type of activity, including network connections, number and type of system calls, failed login attempts, processor usage, and number of e-mails sent. This approach can detect both known and unknown attacks. Lastly, stateful protocol analysis, also known as specification-based detection, compares a vendor-developed profile of specific protocols to current behavior. An example would be monitoring protocol states such as pairing requests and replies. Modi *et al.* [54] provide a survey of IDS techniques used for cloud computing. Many of the approaches use techniques similar to statistical anomaly detection, as well as neural networks and fuzzy logic.

CPS-specific IDS approaches have also been developed. Buttán *et al.* [4] discuss the WSAN4CIP Project which investigated a number of attack detection methods to determine if a sensor node is compromised. The project included intrusion detection and prevention techniques that were adapted to the wireless environment. A microkernel in the sensor node operating system supports multiple levels of security and determines if the code deployed on a sensor node is unchanged. Mitchell *et al.* [55] provide a detailed review of CPS-related IDS research. In addition to IDS, for traditional networked computing systems, CPS IDS monitors both the embedded components and the physical environment, which under attack may exhibit abnormal properties and behavior. However, this is complicated by legacy technology still used in many CPSs. Some legacy components are based on mechanical or hydraulic control with no cyber component, making them difficult to modify or access. Thus CPS IDS must define acceptable component behavior based on sensor readings of the physical environment.

3.5 Data Error Mitigation

Once the anomalous data has been detected it must be mitigated in order to prevent operational disruptions in the CPS. Therefore, it is important that the detection and mitigation process does not hinder normal operation. It is essential that data errors are detected and mitigated, while the data is still viable.

Detected data errors or missing data can be mitigated in a number of ways. In some higher level data cleansing activities, multiple cleansing alternatives are available on a system. In this case, automatic data cleansing requires a set of policies to determine the appropriate option. Mezzanzanica *et al.* [56] present a model-based approach for developing a policy for the data cleansing of a data set. In some cases, data cleansing requires a domain expert to be involved in the data cleansing effort. Gschwandtner *et al.* [57]

present an interactive visual analysis tool called TimeCleanser. This system is designed for data cleansing of time-oriented data. TimeCleanser combines semiautomatic data quality checks and data visualizations to assist the user.

In CPSs, the mitigation technique is additionally dependent on the criticality and valid time interval of the data. Mitigation can be accomplished by correcting, replacing, or ignoring the data error. In many CPS applications, the useful life of a single piece of data is very short making some correction or replacement techniques inappropriate. Additionally, many correction and mitigation techniques require a great deal of computation making the energy consumption prohibitive. However, in other applications, missing and corrupted data minimizes the quality of information and ignoring these errors may cause a serious effect in data analysis.

Gantayat et al. [58] provide a review of research on missing or incomplete data. A variety of techniques are used to generate predicted values. Many of these approaches are very similar to the anomaly detection techniques discussed. The following are approaches for mitigating missing and corrupted data:

- Imputation: This technique replaces missing data values with an estimation based off the data stream's probabilistic model.
- Predicted value imputation: This technique replaces missing data with estimated values based on the data set. The estimation methods vary in complexity from mean or mode values to more complex estimates from training data.
- Distribution-based imputation: This technique replaces missing data using a classification algorithm. A set of pseudo-instances are created when a missing value is encountered. Each pseudo-instance is tested. The replacement value is selected using a weighted comparison.
- Unique value imputation: This technique replaces the missing value using simple substitution from historic information.
- Replacing missing data: This technique replaces the missing data with a value from a test case that resembles the current data set.
- Rough sets: This technique uses lower and upper approximations to determine a replacement value. The benefit of this technique is that there is no need for preliminary or additional information about the data. A number of extensions to rough set have been proposed including tolerance relation, nonsymmetric relation, and valued tolerance relation.
- Similarity relation: This technique replaces the missing data after making a generalized decisions based on the entire data set.

These techniques can be employed to replace corrupted or missing data allowing for correct execution.

4. CLASSIFICATION OF TECHNIQUES BASED ON TYPE OF ANOMALY

In this section we will classify the data cleansing techniques presented in Section 3 based on the type of anomalies each technique is able to detect. Using this classification, we will then discuss where in an ITS each cleansing technique would be most appropriate. In order to classify these techniques, an understanding of various types of data anomalies must be presented.

4.1 Types of Data Anomalies

Jurdak *et al.* [59] classify data anomalies into three broad categories: temporal, spatial, and spatiotemporal. Table 2 contains a summary of these types of anomalies.

Temporal data anomalies are local to one sensor node and can be detected by observing sensor values over time and observing a number of attributes which indicate an error. These attributes include high variability or lack of variability in subsequent sensor readings, gradual reading skews, or out-of-bound and extreme readings. Examples of failures that result in this type of anomaly are as follows. A sensor may fail into a locked state or fail to obtain new samples making the sensor reading remain the same over long periods of time. Another example is as a sensor loses calibration, its data values drift away from the true value resulting in a gradual skew of sensor readings. A major malfunction of the sensor could produce out-of-bound readings that are physically impossible. And lastly, high variability in sensor readings could arise from sensor voltage fluctuations. However, high variability can also result from major changes in the sensed environment. The

Table 2 Summary of Data Anomaly Types

Type of Data Anomaly	Description
Temporal	Temporal anomalies in sensor readings exhibit high variability in subsequent sensor readings, lack of change in sensor readings, gradual reading skews, or out-of-bound readings.
Spatial	Spatial anomalies in sensor readings are significantly different from surrounding nodes' readings.
Spatiotemporal	Spatiotemporal anomalies exhibit a combination of temporal and spatial anomaly attributes. These are rare but difficult to detect.

detection of temporal data anomalies requires the data stream from a single-sensor node as well as stored historical data.

Spatial data anomalies occur when one sensor's data readings are significantly different from the readings of surrounding nodes at a single time period. Detecting this type of anomaly requires a network-aware algorithm. Data redundancy between sensors is exploited to determine which sensors may have faulty readings. This type of detection is only possible for certain types of data with low spatial variation, such as air temperature or humidity. In this type of data, a change in one area will affect the readings of surrounding sensors. Networks with high spatial variation, especially video and audio data, are usually incapable of detecting such anomalies.

Spatiotemporal anomalies combine attributes of both temporal and spatial anomalies. These anomalies are somewhat rare but also more difficult to detect. For example, a storm progressively moving through an area causing sensor nodes to fail would be a spatiotemporal anomaly. Spatiotemporal anomaly detection requires both a network-wide detection algorithm and data streams from multiple sensors.

4.2 Classification of Techniques

A variety of the techniques presented in Section 3 can be employed to detect each of these types of data anomalies. Table 3 contains a summary of the cleansing techniques classified by a detectable anomaly.

Table 3 Classification of Cleansing Approach Based on Type of Anomaly

Cleansing Approaches	Detectable Anomaly
Rule based	Temporal anomalies, if the analysis is performed over a sliding window of recent values. Spatial anomalies, if the analysis is conducted using data from neighboring nodes. Spatiotemporal anomalies cannot be detected due to dimensionality of data.
Estimation based	Temporal and spatial anomalies, if an appropriate probability distribution is used. Spatiotemporal anomalies cannot be detected due to dimensionality of data.
Learning based	Temporal, spatial, and spatiotemporal anomalies, depending on learning or clustering model used.
Behavior based	Not applicable, behavioral detection uses the statistical techniques to analyze system logs or system models of the behavior.

4.2.1 Rule-Based Detection

The detection capability of rule-based statistical approaches depends a great deal on the implementation. The simplest rule-based statistical approach which rejects data if it falls outside of a specified range of acceptable values, determined by the mean and variance of the expected data set, cannot detect temporal, spatial, or spatiotemporal. Simple rule-based anomaly detection can be very effective if the data is well behaved and the rules are set appropriately. However, if the scope of analyzed data is expended even this simple approach can detect temporal and spatial anomalies.

Temporal anomalies can be detected using rule-based statistical approaches if the analysis is performed using a sliding window over a single data stream. The chi-square test performed over a sliding window, outlined in Ngai et al. [41], is able to detect temporal anomalies provided the length of the window and the user-specified acceptable chi-square test level are configured appropriately for the application and the volatility of the data.

Spatial anomalies can be detected using rule-based statistical approaches if the analysis is performed over multiple time-synchronized data streams. The statistical inference approach outlined by Panda et al. [42] uses a voting system based on the calculated mean and variance of a set of neighboring data streams to detect a spatial anomaly.

Spatiotemporal anomalies cannot be detected using rule-based statistical approaches. This is duo to the high dimensionality of data which prevents detection. Rule-based detection approaches are statistical inference techniques which cannot adapt to changing ranges, which are very common in long-term sensor network applications.

4.2.2 Estimation-Based Detection

Estimation-based statistical approaches, which utilize a probability distribution models of the data to detect anomalous values, can detect temporal and spatial anomalies. An example is the detection technique utilizing the ARIMA model proposed by Fang et al. [39]. Temporal anomalies can be detected using the autoregression, integration, and the moving average terms from a single data stream. The new data from that stream is compared with the ARIMA model to determine if the new data is anomalous. Spatial anomalies can be detected by maintaining multiple ARIMA model for all neighboring data streams. The new data is compared with the ARIMA models of neighboring nodes to detect spatial anomalies. Similarly, other detection techniques compare new data with a known pdf or kernel density estimate of a single or neighboring data streams. The limitation of these techniques is how well the data fits the probability distribution. Estimation-based detection, like the rule-based detection, cannot detect spatiotemporal anomalies due to the high dimensionality of data. Unlike rule-based detection approaches, estimation-based approaches can adapt to changing ranges of long-term sensor network applications.

4.2.3 Learning-Based Detection

Learning-based statistical approaches which utilize various data mining clustering and classification algorithms to group data for comparison have very high detection rates of all three types of anomalies [38]. For example, temporal and spatial anomalies can be detected using the neural network based ESN technique described by Chang *et al.* [44] and the Bayesian space–time model proposed by Ni *et al.* [48]. In both cases the network model predicts a data value which is used for comparison. The network model captures the time varying and spatial variation of the data. Another example of more detailed temporal anomaly detection approach is the MSPCA presented by Xie *et al.* [51]. This technique can detect gradual temporal anomalies such as calibration drift and persistent anomalies with different time–frequency features. Spatiotemporal anomalies can be detected using the PCA detection approach proposed by Chitradevi *et al.* [50]. This technique uses PCA to reduce the dimensionality of a data through spectral decomposition. The decomposed data is used to determine the normal behavior in a data set.

4.2.4 Behavioral Detection

Many behavioral approaches utilize the statistical anomaly detection approaches classified above to analyze system behavior rather than sensor or data input. Modi *et al.* [54] and Buttán *et al.* [4] describe techniques which use rule based, estimation based, and learning based to compare system states and detect normal and anomalous behavior. For example, the processor usage of various nodes over time can be compared with mean and variance rules or probability distributions of normal behavior to detect anomalies.

Table 4 Data Anomalies for ITS Static Infrastructure

ITS Element	Type of Data Anomaly
Roadside unit	Requires detection of temporal and spatial anomalies to ensure that the clean data is in database to be used by control elements.
Traffic control	Requires detection of temporal and spatial anomalies to make accurate control decisions.
Central traffic management	Autonomous control elements require basic spatiotemporal anomaly detection in addition to temporal and spatial anomaly detection. Semiautonomous control elements require rigorous spatiotemporal anomaly to detect trends for human in the loop control.

4.3 Static Elements of ITS Infrastructure

In this section the static elements of the example ITS system described in Section 2 will be used to demonstrate where in a CPS each type of data anomalies may be encountered dictating the cleansing technique (Table 4).

4.3.1 Roadside Units

RSUs function as sensor and database nodes, which are queried by control elements in the transportation system and passing vehicles. This makes it essential for clean data to be in the database. The data anomalies likely to be encountered in an RSU are temporal and spatial. A temporal anomaly would be a dramatic change in traffic speed or congestion. This anomaly could be the result of an accident or a faulty sensor. Spatial anomalies would result from multiple RSU communicating and storing duplicated data. This stored information would be compared to detect spatial anomalies collaboratively among neighboring RSU and traffic control systems. However, RSUs do not have a wide enough perspective to detect spatial–temporal. This would require collecting data from many RSUs in a large physical region.

4.3.2 Traffic Signals and Dynamic Lanes

Traffic signals and dynamic lanes have the same functionality of an RSU, including multiple sensors and storage databases, with the addition of a control system. This makes it essential for clean data to be available to the intelligent control system. The data anomalies likely to be encountered are similar to those of the RSU: temporal and spatial. The safety focus of traffic control requires more rigorous detection of these anomalies to ensure safe operation. Spatial–temporal anomalies would not be detectable because of the limited perspective of the environment.

4.3.3 Central Traffic Management

Central traffic management can be divided into the autonomous control elements and semiautonomous control elements. Autonomous control elements would control multiple traffic signals and dynamic lanes for a stretch of road or subdivision. This perspective would necessitate detection of basic spatial–temporal anomalies in addition to temporal and spatial anomalies. Detection and cleansing of spatial–temporal anomalies would be required for detecting trends in failure to better adapt control decisions. An example of this would be a storm or flooding during rush hour causing congestion as well as RSU, traffic light failures from a power outage. As the storm progressed across the area, spatial–temporal anomaly detection would be required to detect failures. The autonomous nature and immediacy of control decisions would limit the complexity of the spatiotemporal anomaly detection.

Semiautonomous control elements would be at a higher level with a human in the loop. At this level, a wide perspective of the road networks and high-level control would necessitate more advanced spatial–temporal anomaly detection. The responsibility of this type of control element would be to detect trends in order to inform specialists. This type of detection is essential for human intervention in the autonomous control and for longer term control decisions and modifications as a part of the design cycle.

4.4 Mobile Elements of ITS Vehicle

In this section, the mobile elements of the example ITS system described in Section 2 will be used to demonstrate where different types of data anomalies may be encountered, as well as the appropriate cleansing techniques for those anomalies (Table 5).

4.4.1 Vehicle Operation

Nodes supporting vehicle operation may experience both spatial and temporal anomalies. From the temporal side, sensors can record values from sensors and identify when values suddenly change. For example, a temperature sensor could track the last three temperature readings, so that it can compare new readings with the average so far. Values that lie outside of the expected range could be considered outliers.

Table 5 Data Anomalies for ITS Mobile Infrastructure

ITS Element	Type of Data Anomaly
Vehicle operation	Temporal anomalies are possible and detectable in data sensed by various on-board sensors. Spatial anomalies may also be possible in cases where the data from several of the same type of sensor may be available.
Navigation	Temporal anomalies in GPS data can be detected and handled. Spatial anomalies are possible depending on the availability of location data from neighboring vehicles.
Driver	Temporal anomalies may arise from sensors assisting automated driving mechanisms, eg, collision avoidance systems. Spatial anomalies may occur when platoons of autonomous vehicles collaborate to make driving decisions.

As for spatial anomalies, a vehicle may rely on several sensors to ascertain the actual state of a sensed environment. For example, on a cold morning, a vehicle may use information from a thermal sensor and four tire pressure sensors to decide whether low pressure in four tires is a result of the weather change or a result of a series of leaks.

4.4.2 Navigation

Anomalies at the navigation level impact the ability of navigation equipment to offer useful advice. Errors in GPS data are extremely common. Navigation equipment should be able to detect temporal errors, where a GPS sensor reports sudden, distant changes in position. In V2V environments, vehicles may collaborate to improve their location accuracy. If surrounding vehicles indicate their location differs, spatial anomalies can be detected and mitigated. Although spatiotemporal anomalies may be possible for navigation, it is less likely to occur and not worth spending resources to identify or mitigate.

4.4.3 Driver

Anomalies at the driver level impact the act of driving. Temporal anomalies may be experienced by systems that have direct control over a vehicle. For example, anomalies from proximity sensors should be detected to allow collision avoidance systems to make timely decisions about steering or braking. Spatial anomalies may also appear as fully autonomous vehicles sense their surroundings and collaborate on driving decisions. Platoons of autonomous vehicles may communicate to make various decisions including braking or lane changing.

5. CLASSIFICATION OF TECHNIQUES BASED ON REQUIREMENTS AND CONSTRAINTS

In this section we will classify the data cleansing techniques presented in Section 3 based on constraints of various elements in the system (Table 6). Using this classification, we will then discuss where in an ITS each cleansing technique would be most appropriate.

5.1 Types of System Constraints

The hardware constraints of a networked system can be evaluated from two perspectives. The first perspective is from the hardware resources of the nodes. Nodes with limited computational resources, including mobile devices, may not capable of executing the same algorithms as more powerful nodes. These nodes may lack the memory or disk space required to execute the algorithm, or they may lack the CPU speeds required to obtain a result in a reasonable amount of time. Additionally, some nodes may have constrained energy resources, which further limits computational ability. Computationally intensive algorithms increase energy consumption and may deplete energy resources at a faster rate.

The second perspective is from the constraints induced by the network. Low-bandwidth or error-prone networks increase the time and energy

Table 6 Summary of Resource Constraints

Type of Resource Constraints	Description
Processing constraints	Constraints on the execution time and processing power required to achieve an appropriate execution time for the cleansing technique.
Storage constraints	Constraints on the storage resources and the size of database needed to store the relevant historical data required to execute the cleansing technique.
Communication constraints	Constraints on the networking requirement. Specifically, these constrains refer to the availability of data from other system components as required by the cleansing technique.
Energy constraints	Constraints on the energy that may be consumed by data cleansing techniques. Both processing and communication tasks may contribute to the overall energy consumption of a node.

spent transmitting data from one node to another. In addition, data corruption may occur as a result of communication over a network. The cleansing technique chosen to inspect data received over a network may vary depending on the nature of the network.

5.1.1 Hardware Resource Constraints

Vyas *et al.* [60] discuss the constraints induced by various hardware architectures of control systems and sensor processing. Evaluating hardware architectures as it pertains to reading sensors, precision in executing a control algorithm, and the time to execute a control algorithm and perform an action with an actuator.

The authors propose an architecture where sensor processing units (SPUs) are able to perform some computations autonomously and communicate sensor data to a primary processor for more complex tasks. The SPUs are configured to continuously execute user-defined functions, which can read data from sensors and perform small computations. As required, the primary CPU on the sensor node can retrieve output from the SPU for use in other tasks. The abilities of SPUs are limited, with respect to the primary CPU on a sensor node. Simple tasks, including reading sensor data and performing basic data fusion, can be accomplished by an SPU. However, more complicated tasks require the intervention of the primary CPU.

For the benefit of devices with limited energy resources, many CPUs support a low-power mode. When the primary CPU is not required, a sensor node could enter a low-power mode to conserve energy. When necessary, SPUs can issue an interrupt to the primary CPU, so that the CPU can perform computations that the sensor device cannot do alone.

Low-power mode may reduce the energy consumption of a sensor node, leading to a longer battery life, but complex data cleansing algorithms running on the primary CPU of a node will still impact the energy resources of that node. With or without the availability of a low-power mode, one may prefer less demanding data cleansing techniques to improve the battery life of sensor nodes. If the data cleansing technique is simple enough, it may be performed by the SPU, further allowing the primary CPU to remain in a low-power state.

5.1.2 Network-Induced Constraints

Zhang *et al.* [61] discuss the constraints induced by the network in a networked control system. A networked control system can be a small scale such as a modern vehicle or a large scale such as a metropolitan power grid.

In both cases, sensors, actuators, and control decision nodes are networked together to create the control system. The network constraints discussed are time delay, packet losses, time-varying transmission intervals, multiple node access issues, and data quantization error. Though these constraints may factor into one's choice of data cleansing technique for a specific application, they are more detailed than required for our discussion on resource constraints for data cleansing techniques. The constraints of the system used for classification of cleansing techniques will be are storage, processing, communication, energy consumption.

5.2 Classification of Techniques

The techniques presented in Section 3 vary in terms of hardware and communication requirements. Table 7 contains a summary of the cleansing techniques classified by a detectable data type.

5.2.1 Rule-Based Detection

Given their simplicity, rule-based cleansing techniques are appropriate to execute on resource-constrained devices. Anomaly detection rules are

Table 7 Classification of Cleansing Approach Based on System Constraints

Cleansing Approach	Resource Constraints
Rule based	Lower processing and storage requirements, when rules are simple. Higher communication costs if the rules rely on data gathered from neighboring nodes. Nodes do not develop models and depend on raw data for anomaly detection.
Estimation based	Requires moderate processing and storage resources to detect anomalies and store statistical models. Communication requirements are lower, however, as statistical models of values seen by neighbors can be stored and reused, instead of relying on raw data.
Learning based	More complex; require more processing and storage resources. Though models can be stored compactly, large quantities of data and extra processing time are required to develop highly effective models.
Behavior based	Requires data from other nodes to capture the state of the system at the expense of additional communication. Historical data can be stored for future reference.

predefined. It is simply a matter of applying those rules to data items to determine whether items fit expectations of data or if they are anomalous. Additionally, the detection of anomalous data is based solely on the set of rules and does not rely on building models of data. With respect to other techniques, rule-based approaches should require fewer CPU and storage resources. As a result, energy consumption may be lower than techniques requiring more complex algorithms. However, as the number and complexity of anomaly detection rules grow, storage, processing, or energy constraints may become problematic.

Communication and energy overhead may increase drastically if detection rules depend on values from neighboring nodes. Raw data collected from neighboring nodes may be used as part of the anomaly detection process. However, rule-based techniques do not maintain models of data that is considered normal. As a result, nodes attempting to identify anomalies based on values sensed by neighbors may incur high communication costs. Matching data aggregated from neighbors is computationally inexpensive, but gathering that data may require significant communication overhead as well as increased energy consumption.

The history maintained by a node may also impact the resource requirements for rule-based cleansing techniques. Nodes that store a long history of raw data for rule-based matching require more storage than those that work with raw data live. This issue is exacerbated by rules that require storing raw data from neighboring nodes. In addition to storage requirements, a longer history of raw data requires increased processing time to arrive at a result and may increase energy consumption as well.

5.2.2 Estimation-Based Detection

Estimation-based techniques require different levels of processing and storage resources to use and store the statistical models that represent normal data. Storage requirements vary depending on the model. Some models can be represented with a few floating-point parameters (eg, Gaussian distribution), while others increase in size as they increase in detail (eg, a histogram). Depending on the cleansing method, extra storage resources may be required to keep several models for data retrieved by local sensors. Some methods may also require storage of models for values retrieved from neighboring nodes as well.

Depending on the complexity of models, more processing resources may be required to determine whether or not data items fit within bounds that models define as normal.

Unlike rule-based techniques, estimation-based techniques do not necessarily need to collect raw data from neighbors to decide whether data items are anomalous. Instead of relying on raw data from neighbors, nodes can store a model for each neighbor that represents the normal values for that neighbor. If the model changes, a node can update its neighbors, so that they may update their stored models accordingly. Periodic model updates should incur less communication overhead than raw data aggregation as well as potentially lower energy consumption.

5.2.3 Learning-Based Detection

Like rule-based techniques, learning-based techniques detect anomalies in raw data. However, they require additional overhead that is not required of rule-based or estimation-based techniques. Learning-based techniques do not require predefined rules nor do they assume that the raw data will fit particular models. Instead, the model of normal data is learned, which leads to highly accurate identification of data anomalies.

This accuracy comes at a cost. Algorithms for learning models can be computationally expensive, increasing processing time and storage while also potentially increasing power consumption. In addition to the resources required to execute learning algorithms, it takes time for the learned model to become accurate enough to be usable. A node's model can be adjusted as it receives new information from its sensors or its neighbors. By including data from neighboring nodes in the learning process, a node may learn its model more quickly. It may also be possible to offload the learning process on more powerful hardware, but this comes at the cost of communication.

Another way to reduce processing overhead is to build a partial model of normal data ahead of time using historically recorded data. However, building a model ahead of time requires making assumptions about data that will be collected. There may be a trade-off between building a flexible, highly accurate model from scratch and reducing the time required to build a useful model.

Once a model is learned, using it to identify anomalies is fast. However, continuing to update the model with the learning algorithms requires additional processing time.

5.2.4 Behavior-Based Detection

Behavior-based detection relies on inspecting previous system states to identify anomalous states. Maintaining historical data incurs larger storage costs as the size of the history grows. However, behavior-based techniques are most applicable at a higher level in a CPS, where nodes are more likely to have reasonable computational and storage resources. These nodes aggregate information about system state from other components in the system. The information retrieved from other system components helps build a system-level view at the cost of processing and communication.

5.3 Static Elements of ITS Infrastructure

In this section the static elements of the example ITS system described in Section 2 will be used to demonstrate where in a CPS the hardware constraints would dictate the cleansing technique (Table 8).

5.3.1 Roadside Units

RSUs are deployed throughout the network making cost the limiting factor. The sensor database nature of an RSU would require a moderate sized storage to facilitate raw data storage of local and neighboring sensor data. However, the data retention policy of the system would dictate the size of storage. The communication requirement of an RSU is very high to facility vehicle and control element access to the data. The processing requirement of an RSU is very low as its primary function is sensor, storage, and communication. Energy efficiency is a concern as installations may be solar/batteries powered. The high communication requirement would require limiting the processing power of the node to meet energy limitations.

Table 8 Resource Constraints for ITS Static Infrastructure

ITS Element	Hardware Constraints
Roadside unit	Highly constrained due to deployment and cost. Requires moderate storage, low processing, and high communication and energy efficiency.
Traffic control	Less limited by cost due to safety critical nature of control. Storage and communication similar to RSU. Requires higher processing to execute control algorithm. Energy efficiency is not an issue.
Central traffic management	Less limited by cost as these are large investments. Very high storage and processing to execute control algorithm. Communication is dependent on granularity of data collected. Energy efficiency is not an issue.

5.3.2 Traffic Signals and Dynamic Lanes

Traffic signals and dynamic lanes have less of a cost limitation the RSU because of the safety critical aspects of their operation. The storage requirements of traffic signals and dynamic lanes would be similar to RSU. The processing and communication requirements of traffic signals and dynamic lanes, however, would be higher than an RSU. The control algorithms used by traffic signals and dynamic lanes require processing and communication to collaboratively make decisions. The short control loop necessitates faster processing. Energy efficiency is not a limitation of these control elements because traffic signals utilize infrastructure power with a battery backup in case of power failure.

5.3.3 Central Traffic Management

Central traffic management elements both autonomous and semiautonomous control elements have similar system constraints. The high-level nature of these nodes means cost is less of a limiting factor. These control elements will require the most processing power and storage. The control algorithms in a central traffic management system would utilize the most data both current and historical. Communication requirement will be dependent on the amount of raw data collected by the node. The communication requirement would be limited if only aggregated data was collected and database queries were execute in the sensor database nodes. Energy efficiency is not really an issue for central traffic management aside from the cost associated with a higher energy bill.

5.4 Mobile Elements of ITS Vehicle

In this section the mobile elements of the example ITS system described in Section 2 will be used to demonstrate where in a CPS the resource constraints would dictate the cleansing technique (Table 9).

5.4.1 Vehicle Operation

Sensors for vehicle operation are typically embedded systems and are not as computationally sophisticated as other components of the vehicle. Although their processing power may be lower, these components should still be able to clean data items very quickly. Simpler data cleansing techniques, like rule-based techniques, can cleanse data to some degree with short execution times without requiring more advanced CPUs. Communication for these elements is short distance, due to the proximity of the devices.

Table 9 Resource Constraints for ITS Mobile Infrastructure

ITS Element	Resource Constraints
Vehicle operation	Constrained processing and storage resources. Limited, short range communication. Depending on location, limited energy resources.
Navigation	Less constrained, though still limited, processing and storage. More capable communication for V2V or V2I.
Driver	Less constrained, though still limited, processing. Requires rapid response for safety critical decisions. May include heavy communication load for fully autonomous vehicle coordination.

5.4.2 Navigation

Navigation equipment tends to be more capable than the embedded devices responsible for sensing vehicle state. These devices must be capable of interacting with a human user, sometimes approaching a PC-level user experience. They are designed with a fair amount of disk space and reasonably fast processors. In applications where V2V communication is required, communication may be heavy.

Because of their access to more capable computational resources, navigation equipment may perform more sophisticated data cleansing techniques. Learning-based techniques can be used to detect anomalies in GPS data [62], which can be performed by navigation equipment.

5.4.3 Driver

Control decisions that affect driving should be based on accurate information and action should happen quickly. To meet these goals, data anomalies should be identified quickly to permit a fast control response. Considering the safety implications of systems like collision avoidance, it makes sense that manufacturers would invest in more powerful equipment to process decisions. Higher performance processors and more storage enable more advanced cleansing techniques, like behavior based and learning based.

For fully autonomous vehicles, communication may be heavy as well. The vehicle may consider information gathered from neighboring vehicles when preparing to make a control decision.

6. CLASSIFICATION OF TECHNIQUES BASED ON TYPE OF DATA

In this section we will classify the data cleansing techniques presented in Section 3 based on the type of data that can be cleansed by each approach.

Using this classification, we will then discuss where in an ITS each cleansing technique would be most appropriate.

6.1 Types of Data

The types of data that will used for classification are numerical and categorical data [63]. Statistical analysis, which data mining is rooted in, also recognizes additional data types including binary, ordinal, binomial, count, additive, and multiplicative. These statistical data types can be mapped to numerical or categorical data types because their distinguishing characteristics are not relevant to a control system in a CPS.

Numerical data types are any kind of quantitative data including any data that can have a number associated with it suitable for ranking. Numerical data can be discrete or continuous values describing absolute or relative measurements. Discrete data represents items that can be counted such as number of cars waiting at a stop light or the number of lanes that are open in a tunnel. A computer system would store this type of data as integer values. Continuous data represents measurement data such as the average speed of vehicles on a certain road. A computer system would store this type of data as floating-point values. Numerical data is the most common type of data in a control system.

Categorical data types are qualitative in nature. Categorical data is data that represents characteristics such as the status of a road segment (open, closed) or an identification tag such as a license plate number. This type of data also includes binary or true/false data. System states are considered categorical data, for example, the status of a traffic light (green, red, yellow). In a computer system this type of data can be stored as strings or as enumerations.

6.2 Classification of Techniques

A variety of the techniques presented in Section 3 can be employed to analyze and detect anomalies in each of these types of data. Table 10 contains a summary of the cleansing techniques classified by a detectable data type.

6.2.1 Rule- and Estimation-Based Detection

Rule-based and estimation-based detection approaches are similar enough to consider them as a single class from the data type point of view. Only the simplest rule-base detection approach is relevant for categorical data. This detection may include checking incoming data describing the state

Table 10 Classification of Cleansing Approach Based on Data Type

Cleansing Approaches	Applicable Data Type
Rule based & Estimation-Based	Ideal for purely numerical data. Unable to detect anomalies in categorical beyond the simplest validity check of a rule-based approach.
Learning based	Ideally suited for purely numerical data and combinations of categorical and numeric data. Unable to detect anomalies in purely categorical data.
Behavior based	Able to detect anomalies in numerical data extracted from system logs. Ideal for system state categorical data using stateful analysis.

of a neighboring system is in fact an acceptable state, eg, "blue" is not an state of a traffic light. Beyond this simple detection, anomalies in categorical data cannot be detected by rule- or estimation-based approaches. This is because both require relative distances for comparison of data values. The mean and variance of a system state is irrelevant. However, strictly categorical data without any order/ranking is not a realistic scenario for a CPS control system. Numerical data, however, is specifically what these detection techniques are designed for.

6.2.2 Learning-Based Detection

Learning-based detection approach suffers from the same limitation as rule- and estimation-based approaches in terms of detecting anomalies in purely categorical data. The statistical nature of learning-based detection makes them very powerful for numerical data anomalies with capabilities beyond those of rule- and estimation-base approaches.

Learning-base detection has the added capability of detecting anomalies using a combination of categorical and numerical data. An example of this would be a data packet containing the state of a stop light, categorical data, and sensor measurements from traffic flow in the various directions around the light. Clustering approaches can be used to determine outlines based on this state and numerical data.

6.2.3 Behavior-Based Detection

Behavior-based detection approaches are ideally suited for numerical, categorical, and the combination of categorical and numerical data. Numerical data extracted from system events can be analyzed using the statistical detection approaches above to detect anomalies. System events may include any type of logged activity such as network number and type of system calls, processor usage, and number of packets sent or received by a node.

However, behavioral detection techniques are ideal for categorical and combined numerical and categorical data. For example, stateful protocol analysis described by Liao *et al.* [53]. In this approach, the present system state and the sequence of historical system states are compared to an expected system operation profile. Numerical data can be used in addition to the sequence of system states to compare against a system model. An anomaly is detected when the system deviates from the behavior of the model.

6.3 Static Elements of ITS Infrastructure

In this section the static elements of the example ITS system described in Section 2 will be used to demonstrate where in a CPS each data type is encountered dictating the cleansing technique (Table 11).

6.3.1 Roadside Units

The primary data type processed by RSUs is numerical. Examples of sensors used by RSU are loop detector counts, traffic video, acoustical, and in-road magnetic sensors. In all cases, numerical data is extracted to capture the state of traffic in the sensed area.

Categorical data is also collected by RSU such as vehicle identification number or tag. These tags can be either transmitted to the RSU by the vehicle or gathered from the air such as Bluetooth packets transmitted by a cellular phone in passing vehicles. Numerical data is extracted from this categorical data though collaboration between RSU, eg, detecting speed by comparing time stamps of sequential RSU on a road segment. Numerical data is the primary data type collected and stored by an RSU.

Table 11 Data Types for ITS Static Infrastructure

ITS Element	Type of Data
Roadside unit	Primarily numerical data and numerical data extracted from categorical data.
Traffic control	Primarily numerical data with the addition of controller state categorical data of neighboring controllers.
Central traffic management	Both numerical and categorical data collected from RSU and traffic signals and dynamic lanes.

6.3.2 Traffic Signals and Dynamic Lanes

Traffic signals and dynamic lanes process the same data types as RSU with the addition of categorical data. The categorical data is the sequential control states of the controller and the controllers neighbors. Access to both numerical and categorical data facilitates more rigorous behavioral detection of the control system and its neighbors.

6.3.3 Central Traffic Management

Central traffic management process both controller state-based categorical data and numerical data gathered from sensors. Autonomous and semiautonomous central traffic management will process this type of data to detect anomalies in the traffic signals and dynamic lanes system states utilizing the numerical data provided by RSU.

6.4 Mobile Elements of ITS Vehicle

A variety of the techniques presented in Section 3 can be employed to analyze and detect anomalies in each of these types of data. Table 12 contains a summary of the cleansing techniques classified by a detectable data type.

6.4.1 Vehicle Operation

Most sensor readings that facilitate vehicle operation are numerical. Various temperature and pressure sensors retrieve numerical values that can be scaled or otherwise modified. Categorical measurements do not apply to this area.

6.4.2 Navigation

Navigation equipment relies on numerical values as well. GPS data, such as time, longitude, and latitude, can be retrieved and cleaned. Congestion data may be retrieved from I2V or V2V communication and can be represented as a measurement of the amount of traffic flowing through a road segment. Categorical measurements do not apply to this area.

Table 12 Data Types for ITS Mobile Infrastructure

ITS Element	Type of Data Anomaly
Vehicle operation	Numerical
Navigation	Numerical
Driver	Numerical and categorical

6.4.3 Driver

Numerical sensor readings from proximity sensors may facilitate decisions made by autonomous and semiautonomous vehicles. Additionally, categorical data may be available by inspecting messages received by other vehicles in the ITS. Consider a situation where a vehicle informs its neighbors of its intention to change lanes. However, the vehicle never executes the lane change. This ITS equivalent of leaving ones blinker on could be detected as an anomaly, so that other vehicles can resume normal traffic behavior.

7. CLASSIFICATION OF TECHNIQUES BASED ON HIERARCHICAL LOCATION

In this section we will classify the data cleansing techniques presented in Section 3 based on the hierarchical nature the system. Using this classification, we will then discuss where in an ITS each cleansing technique would be most appropriate.

7.1 Levels of System Hierarchy

Elements of an ITS can be categorized based on their location within the overall ITS hierarchy. Sensors are at the base of the hierarchy. They are capable of acquiring data and may have limited access to resources. The sensor actuator level of the hierarchy is above the sensor level. Sensor actuators are able to make some control decisions based on data acquired from local sensors. Next, the control level uses data collected by sensors and sensor actuators to make control decisions at a wider scope. Finally, the supervisor level encompasses human operator or supervisors who make decisions based on data retrieved from lower levels of the hierarchy. The retrieved data may be processed prior to use as the basis of decisions.

The sensor level of the hierarchy is the base, as it provides a foundation for the autonomous control decisions made by other levels in the hierarchy. Members of this level, such as RSUs, are capable of collecting data from local sensors and disseminating values to others. Sensors are unable to make control decisions; they simply acquire and allow access to data items.

Because their role is simple, sensor-level devices can use more simplistic data cleaning techniques. Rule-based techniques, for example, are simple to apply and can remove obviously erroneous data items. Estimation-based techniques may be applicable, as well, depending on the data being sensed.

At the sensor actuator level, local sensors are used to facilitate control decisions. For example, a traffic light might use in-road sensors or traffic cameras to control the flow of traffic at an intersection. Because these devices have some control over the infrastructure, they should be more capable machines with more resources than a sensor-level device. With access to better resources than a sensor-level device, sensor actuators can make use of more sophisticated data cleansing techniques.

For example, estimation-based techniques are more sophisticated than rule-based techniques, but they are still fast for applications that rely on short execution times. Learning-based techniques may also be feasible on sensor actuators. More capable hardware allows for more advanced algorithms (eg, machine learning), which may be worth the additional costs to achieve more accurate anomaly detection. Sensor actuators may also make use of behavioral-based methods to verify its own behavior and check that its control loop leads to acceptable states.

Control-level devices use data from sensors and sensor actuators to make control decisions for a complete road section that may have multiple lights or dynamic lanes. These devices have a larger scope of responsibility. As a result, more sophisticated methods are appropriate. Anomaly detection and data cleansing should be accurate to ensure decisions are made based on accurate data. Behavior-based and learning-based methods seem the most appropriate. Estimation-based methods may also fit, provided that there is a well developed, high-level model for identifying anomalous data items. Control-level devices have a wider scope of influence. As a result, they have more time to spend analyzing data and arrive at decisions.

The top of the hierarchy, the supervisor level, includes a central office with human operator/supervisor. Decisions made at this level affect the state of the system, as well as future design cycle decisions. Data may be interpreted by a human to aid in the design process. The most sophisticated cleansing techniques, ie, learning-based and behavior-based, are appropriate for this level. Although data may be interpreted by a human, it is important for results to be accurate considering the broad impact that decisions have at this level.

7.2 Classification of Techniques

7.2.1 Static Elements of ITS Infrastructure

In this section the static elements of the example ITS system described in Section 2 will be used to demonstrate where in a CPS the hierarchical location would dictate the cleansing technique (Table 13).

Table 13 Hierarchical Location for ITS Static Infrastructure

ITS Element	Hierarchical Location
Roadside unit	Operate at the sensor level without direct influence over the state of the system.
Traffic control	Operate at the sensor actuator level with the ability the sense the environment and influence the state of traffic on a road or at a traffic light.
Central traffic management	The autonomous traffic management units operate at the control level. The high level, human in the loop, semiautonomous traffic management units operate at the supervisor level.

7.2.1.1 Roadside Units

RSUs function at the sensor level without direct influence over the sensed area. The data transmitted by RSU can influence the decisions of intelligent vehicles utilizing I2V communication. However, this is not considered actuation in the environment because the vehicles are not directly controlled by the RSU.

7.2.1.2 Traffic Signals and Dynamic Lanes

In addition to sensor capabilities for sensing traffic in a local area, traffic signals and dynamic lanes have direct control over a lane or a traffic interchange. This means that the traffic signals and dynamic lanes operate at the sensor actuator level.

7.2.1.3 Central Traffic Management

Central traffic management units operate at the control level and the supervisor level. The intermediate autonomous traffic management units operate at the control level. The autonomous traffic management units have control over traffic signals and dynamic lanes without directly controlling the state. An example of this would be alleviating a traffic congestion in an area by directing dynamic lanes and traffic signals that feed the congested area in order to slow incoming traffic. This level of traffic management does not directly control the changing of a traffic light. It has a higher level of control.

The highest level of control is the human-in-the-loop, semiautonomous traffic management units that operate at the supervisor level. This level of operation is more focused on long-term control and design cycle control rather than immediate control decisions. However, in an emergency the supervisory control can directly take over lower level control systems to mitigate a failure.

7.3 Mobile Elements of ITS Vehicle

In this section the mobile elements of the example ITS system described in Section 2 will be used to demonstrate where in a CPS the hierarchical location would dictate the cleansing technique (Table 14).

7.3.1 Vehicle Operation

Sensors that support vehicle operations are at the sensor level. Tire pressure sensors, for example, can report the status of tires, but are unable to perform any action based on the state. Rain sensors and light sensors, on the other hand, are able to sense conditions and perform an action as a result, namely starting windshield wipers or turning on head lamps.

7.3.2 Navigation

In an autonomous vehicle, the navigation system plays an important role in driving decisions made by the vehicle. For this type of vehicle, the navigation system plays the role of a sensor, in that it determines its current location. However, the navigation recommendations are used to control the routes driven. In a way, the navigation system also acts as a sensor actuator. Its recommendations can be viewed as commands for driving to a particular destination.

Semiautonomous vehicles may have collision avoidance or other driving control systems. In this case, the navigation system acts at the supervisor level. The driver makes the decision about changes to navigation based on the recommendations of the navigation system.

Table 14 Hierarchical Location for ITS Mobile Infrastructure

ITS Element	Location of Component
Vehicle operation	Takes place at the sensor or the sensor actuator level. Some devices simply gather data, while others are able to take action based on locally sensed information.
Navigation	Takes place at the sensor or supervisor level. While autonomous vehicles can use the navigation information to directly control driving behavior, other vehicles relay navigation data to a human driver, who ultimately decides on the chosen route.
Driver	Takes place at the controller or supervisor level. Autonomous vehicles use sensor data to directly control the path of the vehicle, while other vehicles rely on a driver to interpret and act on sensed information.

7.3.3 Driver

For autonomous vehicles, the human passenger has limited abilities to intervene with driving. Their ability to interact with a vehicle is strictly at a supervisor level. A vehicle may inform the user of diagnostic concerns, but control is ultimately left to the vehicle itself.

Semiautonomous vehicles, on the other hand, permit humans to drive. Although some automated systems, such as collision avoidance, can momentarily intervene and take control, the driver is in control of the vehicle. In this case, the collision avoidance system acts at the controller level. It autonomously acts to avoid dangerous situations. Otherwise, the driver acts as a supervisor. They are able to interpret results and take appropriate action behind the wheel.

8. CONCLUSION

Modern critical infrastructure cyber-physical systems are designed to meet very high performance standards. This is only achievable using sophisticated intelligent autonomous control systems which are extremely data dependent. Therefore, it is essential to provide accurate real-time data to the control system. When these systems are deployed in extremely unpredictable environments it is essential that data cleansing is used to minimize the potential failures that would result from control systems processing erroneous data.

In this survey we discussed the sources of corrupted data and various general purpose data cleansing techniques including detection and mitigation methods. We classify these techniques based on their applicability to CPSs specifically discussing the anomalies which can be detected, hardware constraints of various nodes within a CPS, type of data being processed, and hierarchical location within a CPS. Understanding the limitations of various data cleansing technique is essential to designing fault tolerant and survivable CPSs. We are working to model the extent to which data errors can propagate with in a CPS. Specifically looking at the effect of data cleansing within a system. This information will be essential to designing robust CPSs.

GLOSSARY

CPS Critical infrastructure cyber-physical systems
ESN Echo state network
I2V Infrastructure to vehicle communication
IDS Intrusion detection systems

ITS Intelligent transportation systems
MSPCA Multiscale principal component analysis
PCA Principal component analysis
pdf Probability distribution function
RSU Roadside unit
TQDM Total Quality Data Management
V2I Vehicle to infrastructure communication
V2V Vehicle to vehicle communication
V2X Vehicle to everything communication

REFERENCES

[1] P. Derler, E.A. Lee, A.S. Vincentelli, Modeling cyber physical systems, Proc. IEEE 100 (1) (2012) 13–28.
[2] D.E. Bakken, A. Bose, C.H. Hauser, D.E. Whitehead, G.C. Zweigle, Smart generation and transmission with coherent, real-time data, Proc. IEEE 99 (6) (2011) 928–951.
[3] B.A. Hoverstad, A. Tidemann, H. Langseth, Effects of data cleansing on load prediction algorithms, in: 2013 IEEE Symposium on Computational Intelligence Applications in Smart Grid (CIASG), IEEE, Singapore, 2013, pp. 93–100.
[4] L. Buttyán, D. Gessner, A. Hessler, P. Langendoerfer, Application of wireless sensor networks in critical infrastructure protection: challenges and design options [security and privacy in emerging wireless networks], IEEE Wireless Commun. 17 (5) (2010) 44–49.
[5] A.A. Kirilenko, A.W. Lo, Moore's law versus Murphy's law: algorithmic trading and its discontents, J. Econ. Perspect. 27 (2) (2013) 51–72.
[6] B. Miller, D. Rowe, A survey of SCADA and critical infrastructure incidents, in: Proceedings of the 1st Annual Conference on Research in Information Technology, ACM, New York, NY, 2012, pp. 51–56.
[7] A. Berizzi, The Italian 2003 blackout, in: IEEE Power Engineering Society General Meeting, IEEE, Denver, CO, 2004, pp. 1673–1679.
[8] S.V. Buldyrev, R. Parshani, G. Paul, H.E. Stanley, S. Havlin, Catastrophic cascade of failures in interdependent networks, Nature 464 (7291) (2010) 1025–1028.
[9] M. Woodard, S.S. Sarvestani, A.R. Hurson, A survey of research on data corruption in cyber-physical critical infrastructure systems, Adv. Comput. 98 (2015) 59–87.
[10] I.B.M. Solutions, Delivering intelligent transport systems driving integration and innovation, Tech. rep., IBM Corporation, 2007.
[11] R.R. Rajkumar, I. Lee, L. Sha, J. Stankovic, Cyber-physical systems: the next computing revolution, in: Proceedings of the 47th Design Automation Conference, ACM, 2010, pp. 731–736.
[12] M. Amadeo, C. Campolo, A. Molinaro, Information-centric networking for connected vehicles: a survey and future perspectives, Commun. Mag. IEEE 54 (2) (2016) 98–104.
[13] K.N. Qureshi, A.H. Abdullah, A survey on intelligent transportation systems, Middle-East J. Sci. Res. 15 (5) (2013) 629–642.
[14] I.F. Akyildiz, W. Su, Y. Sankarasubramaniam, E. Cayirci, A survey on sensor networks, IEEE Commun. Mag. 40 (8) (2002) 102–114.
[15] A.R. Hurson, Y. Jiao, Database system architecture—a walk through time: from centralized platform to mobile computing-keynote address, Advanced Distributed Systems, Springer, Guadalajara, Mexico, 2005, pp. 1–9.
[16] P. Bonnet, J. Gehrke, P. Seshadri, Towards sensor database systems, in: Mobile Data Management, Springer, Hong Kong, China, 2001, pp. 3–14.

[17] N. Tsiftes, A. Dunkels, A database in every sensor, in: Proceedings of the 9th ACM Conference on Embedded Networked Sensor Systems, ACM, New York, NY, USA, 2011, pp. 316–332.

[18] G. Dimitrakopoulos, P. Demestichas, Intelligent transportation systems, Vehicular Technol. Mag. IEEE 5 (1) (2010) 77–84.

[19] L. Li, D. Wen, D. Yao, A survey of traffic control with vehicular communications, IEEE Trans. Intell. Transport. Syst. 15 (1) (2014) 425–432.

[20] V. Milanes, J. Villagra, J. Godoy, J. Simo, J. Perez, E. Onieva, An intelligent V2I-based traffic management system, IEEE Trans. Intell. Transport. Syst. 13 (1) (2012) 49–58.

[21] E. Rahm, H.H. Do, Data cleaning: problems and current approaches, IEEE Data Eng. Bull. 23 (4) (2000) 3–13.

[22] J.I. Maletic, A. Marcus, Data cleansing: beyond integrity analysis, in: IQ Citeseer, 2000, pp. 200–209.

[23] L. Bertossi, S. Kolahi, L.V. Lakshmanan, Data cleaning and query answering with matching dependencies and matching functions, Theory Comput. Syst. 52 (3) (2013) 441–482.

[24] R.Y. Wang, A product perspective on total data quality management, Commun. ACM 41 (2) (1998) 58–65.

[25] M. Dallachiesa, A. Ebaid, A. Eldawy, A. Elmagarmid, I.F. Ilyas, M. Ouzzani, N. Tang, NADEEF: a commodity data cleaning system, in: Proceedings of the 2013 ACM SIGMOD International Conference on Management of Data, ACM, New York, NY, 2013, pp. 541–552.

[26] M. Budka, M. Eastwood, B. Gabrys, P. Kadlec, M.M. Salvador, S. Schwan, A. Tsakonas, I. žliobaitė, From sensor readings to predictions: on the process of developing practical soft sensors, Advances in Intelligent Data Analysis XIII, Springer, Leuven, Belgium, 2014, pp. 49–60.

[27] A. Aviźienis, J.-C. Laprie, B. Randell, C. Landwehr, Basic concepts and taxonomy of dependable and secure computing, IEEE Trans. Depend. Secure Comput. 1 (1) (2004) 11–33.

[28] Y. Mo, T.-H. Kim, K. Brancik, D. Dickinson, H. Lee, A. Perrig, B. Sinopoli, Cyber-physical security of a smart grid infrastructure, Proc. IEEE 100 (1) (2012) 195–209.

[29] S. Amin, X. Litrico, S.S. Sastry, A.M. Bayen, Stealthy deception attacks on water SCADA systems, in: Proceedings of the 13th ACM International Conference on Hybrid Systems: Computation and Control, ACM, Stockholm, Sweden, 2010, pp. 161–170.

[30] J.L. Cebula, L.R. Young, A taxonomy of operational cyber security risks, Tech. rep., DTIC Document, 2010.

[31] C.C. Aggarwal, N. Ashish, A. Sheth, The Internet of things: a survey from the data-centric perspective, Managing and Mining Sensor Data, Springer, New York, NY, 2013, pp. 383–428.

[32] S. Rajasegarar, C. Leckie, M. Palaniswami, Anomaly detection in wireless sensor networks, IEEE Wireless Commun. 15 (4) (2008) 34–40.

[33] S. Yin, G. Wang, H.R. Karimi, Data-driven design of robust fault detection system for wind turbines, Mechatronics 24 (4) (2014) 298–306.

[34] P. Freeman, P. Seiler, G.J. Balas, Air data system fault modeling and detection, Control Eng. Pract. 21 (10) (2013) 1290–1301.

[35] L.-A. Tang, X. Yu, S. Kim, Q. Gu, J. Han, A. Leung, T. La Porta, Trustworthiness analysis of sensor data in cyber-physical systems, J. Comput. Syst. Sci. 79 (3) (2013) 383–401.

[36] Y. Zhang, N. Meratnia, P. Havinga, Outlier detection techniques for wireless sensor networks: a survey, IEEE Commun. Surv. Tutor. 12 (2) (2010) 159–170.

[37] V. Chandola, A. Banerjee, V. Kumar, Anomaly detection: a survey, ACM Comput. Surv. (CSUR) 41 (3) (2009) 15.

[38] L. Fang, S. Dobson, In-network sensor data modelling methods for fault detection, Evolving Ambient Intelligence, Springer, Dublin, Ireland, 2013, pp. 176–189.

[39] L. Fang, S. Dobson, Unifying sensor fault detection with energy conservation, Self-Organizing Systems, Springer, Palma de Mallorca, Spain, 2014, pp. 176–181.

[40] B. Bilir, A. Abur, Bad data processing when using the coupled measurement model and Takahashi's sparse inverse method, in: Innovative Smart Grid Technologies Conference Europe (ISGT-Europe), 2014 IEEE PES, IEEE, Istanbul, Turkey, 2014, pp. 1–5.

[41] E.C.H. Ngai, J. Liu, M.R. Lyu, On the intruder detection for sinkhole attack in wireless sensor networks, in: IEEE International Conference on Communications, ICC'06, vol. 8, 2006, pp. 3383–3389.

[42] M. Panda, P.M. Khilar, An efficient fault detection algorithm in wireless sensor network, in: Contemporary Computing, Springer, Noida, India, 2011, pp. 279–288.

[43] S. Rajasegarar, C. Leckie, M. Palaniswami, J.C. Bezdek, Distributed anomaly detection in wireless sensor networks, in: 10th IEEE Singapore International Conference on Communication systems, ICCS 2006, IEEE, Singapore, 2006, pp. 1–5.

[44] M. Chang, A. Terzis, P. Bonnet, Mote-based online anomaly detection using echo state networks, Dstributed Computing in Sensor Systems, Springer, Marina del Rey, CA, 2009, pp. 72–86.

[45] O. Obst, Distributed backpropagation-decorrelation learning, in: NIPS Workshop: Large-Scale Machine Learning: Parallelism and Massive Datasets, 2009.

[46] C. Mayfield, J. Neville, S. Prabhakar, ERACER: a database approach for statistical inference and data cleaning, in: Proceedings of the 2010 ACM SIGMOD International Conference on Management of data, ACM, Indianapolis, IN, 2010, pp. 75–86.

[47] X.R. Wang, J.T. Lizier, O. Obst, M. Prokopenko, P. Wang, Spatiotemporal anomaly detection in gas monitoring sensor networks, in: Wireless Sensor Networks, Proceeding of the 5th European Conference, EWSN 2008, Bologna, Italy, January 30–February 1, 2008, pp. 90–105, vol. 4913,□Bologna, Italy.

[48] K. Ni, G. Pottie, Sensor network data fault detection with maximum a posteriori selection and Bayesian modeling, ACM Trans. Sensor Netw. (TOSN) 8 (3) (2012) 23.

[49] J.W. Branch, C. Giannella, B. Szymanski, R. Wolff, H. Kargupta, In-network outlier detection in wireless sensor networks, Knowledge Inform. Syst. 34 (1) (2013) 23–54.

[50] N. Chitradevi, V. Palanisamy, K. Baskaran, U.B. Nisha, Outlier aware data aggregation in distributed wireless sensor network using robust principal component analysis, in: 2010 International Conference on Computing Communication and Networking Technologies (ICCCNT), IEEE, Karur, India, 2010, pp. 1–9.

[51] Y.-x. Xie, X.-g. Chen, J. Zhao, Data fault detection for wireless sensor networks using multi-scale PCA method, in: 2nd International Conference on Artificial Intelligence, Management Science and Electronic Commerce (AIMSEC), 2011, IEEE, 2011, pp. 7035–7038.

[52] E.U. Warriach, T.A. Nguyen, M. Aiello, K. Tei, A hybrid fault detection approach for context-aware wireless sensor networks, in: IEEE 9th International Conference on Mobile Ad Hoc and Sensor Systems (MASS), 2012, IEEE, 2012, pp. 281–289.

[53] H.-J. Liao, C.-H. Richard Lin, Y.-C. Lin, K.-Y. Tung, Intrusion detection system: a comprehensive review, J. Netw. Comput. Appl. 36 (1) (2013) 16–24.

[54] C. Modi, D. Patel, B. Borisaniya, H. Patel, A. Patel, M. Rajarajan, A survey of intrusion detection techniques in cloud, J. Netw. Comput. Appl. 36 (1) (2013) 42–57.

[55] R. Mitchell, I.-R. Chen, A survey of intrusion detection techniques for cyber-physical systems, ACM Comput. Surv. (CSUR) 46 (4) (2014) 55.

[56] M. Mezzanzanica, R. Boselli, M. Cesarini, F. Mercorio, A model-based approach for developing data cleansing solutions, J. Data Inform. Q. 5 (4) (2015) 13.

[57] T. Gschwandtner, W. Aigner, S. Miksch, J. Gärtner, S. Kriglstein, M. Pohl, N. Suchy, TimeCleanser: a visual analytics approach for data cleansing of time-oriented data, in: Proceedings of the 14th International Conference on Knowledge Technologies and Data-driven Business, ACM, Graz, Austria, 2014, p. 18.

[58] S.S. Gantayat, A. Misra, B.S. Panda, A study of incomplete data–a review, in: Proceedings of the International Conference on Frontiers of Intelligent Computing: Theory and Applications (FICTA) 2013, Springer, 2014, pp. 401–408.

[59] R. Jurdak, X.R. Wang, O. Obst, P. Valencia, Wireless sensor network anomalies: diagnosis and detection strategies, Intellgence-Based Systems Engineering, Springer, 2011, pp. 309–325.

[60] S. Vyas, A. Gupte, C.D. Gill, R.K. Cytron, J. Zambreno, P.H. Jones, Hardware architectural support for control systems and sensor processing, ACM Trans. Embed. Comput. Syst. 13 (2) (2013) 16:1–16:25.

[61] L. Zhang, H. Gao, O. Kaynak, Network-induced constraints in networked control Systems: a survey, IEEE Trans. Indus. Inform. 9 (1) (2013) 403–416.

[62] J.-A. Ting, E. Theodorou, S. Schaal, Machine Learning: ECML 2007: 18th European Conference on Machine Learning, Warsaw, Poland, September 17–21, Proceedings, Learning an Outlier-Robust Kalman Filter, Springer Berlin Heidelberg, Berlin, Heidelberg, 2007, pp. 748–756. ISBN 978-3-540-74958-5.

[63] I.H. Witten, E. Frank, Data Mining: Practical Machine Learning Tools and Techniques, Morgan Kaufmann, Burlington, MA, 2005.

ABOUT THE AUTHORS

Mark Woodard received a B.S. degree in Electrical and Computer Engineering from the Virginia Military Institute in 2008. He is currently a Ph.D. candidate in Computer Engineering at the Missouri University of Science and Technology, where he is a GAANN Fellow. His research interests include data interdependence, survivability, and modeling critical infrastructure cyber-physical systems. Mark is a member of IEEE and Tau Beta Pi.

Michael Wisely received the B.S. degree in Computer Science and Computer Engineering from the Missouri University of Science and Technology in 2012. He is currently a Ph.D. candidate in Computer Science at Missouri S&T, where he is a GAANN Fellow and a Chancellor's Fellow. His research interests include traffic modeling and distributed computing. Michael is a member of IEEE and ACM.

Sahra Sedigh Sarvestani received the B.S.E.E. degree from Sharif University of Technology in 1995, and the M.S.E.E. and Ph.D. degrees from Purdue University, in 1998 and 2003, respectively. She subsequently joined the Missouri University of Science and Technology, where she is currently an Associate Professor of Electrical and Computer Engineering. Her research centers on development and modeling of dependable networks and systems, with focus on critical infrastructure. She is a Fellow of the National Academy of Engineering's Frontiers of Engineering Education Program and held a Purdue Research Foundation Fellowship from 1996 to 2000. She is a member of HKN and ACM and a senior member of the IEEE.

CHAPTER FOUR

Indexing and Querying Techniques for Moving Objects in Both Euclidean Space and Road Network

L. Heendaliya, M. Wisely, D. Lin, S. Sedigh Sarvestani, A. Hurson
Missouri University of Science and Technology, Rolla, MO, United States

Contents

Abstract

Location-dependent query is a service that enables users to acquire real-time location-dependent information on mobile objects. This type of service is challenged by the size and volatility of the underlying data. This challenge has created the need for new methods that allow users to efficiently access, retrieve, and update volatile mobile object data. Motivated by this necessity, this chapter explores and discusses research challenges and issues regarding indexing and querying mobile data. The support for

Advances in Computers, Volume 102
ISSN 0065-2458
http://dx.doi.org/10.1016/bs.adcom.2016.05.003

predictive queries on road-network constrained mobile objects is a major deficiency in the existing research. This chapter also presents performance evaluation on some solutions of indexing mobile objects as well as their supported predictive queries under the road-network constraints.

ABBREVIATIONS

ANR-tree adaptive network R-tree
AU adaptive unit
BS base station
BP-tree binary partition tree
CPS cyber physical system
DIME disposable index for moving objects
GTR group update time parameter R-tree
GPS global positioning system
INOR-tree intersection-oriented network R-tree
KNNQ K nearest neighbor query
LAQ location aware query
LDQ location-dependent query
MO moving object
MBR minimum bounding rectangle
MQM monitoring query management
MOVNet MOVing objects in road networks
NNQ nearest neighbor query
PLQ predictive line query
QI query indexing
RKNNQ reverse K nearest neighbor query
RQ range query
RUM-tree R-tree with update memo
SO solo object
SQM spatial query management
STRIPES scalable trajectory index for predicted positions in moving object databases
TPR-tree time parameterized R-tree

1. INTRODUCTION

The Consumer Electronics Association estimated that over 15 million stand-alone global positioning systems (GPSs) were sold in 2009. This estimation did not include GPS units embedded in vehicles or mobile devices, such as phones and iPads. This increasing trend in technology has inspired a series of new services intended to address people's social and societal needs.

Acquiring real-time traffic information, providing the shortest detoured path, and finding the closest hospital or gas station are few examples of such services.

Both economy and safety are primary motivators behind these services. At least 35% of the working population in the United States commutes more than 30 min each day [1]. Additionally, Americans wasted approximately 4.2 billion hours and $87.2 billion in fuel while stuck in traffic in 2009 alone [2]. Less time wasted on the road results more time for productive activities and reduced travel spending. Furthermore, less time spent in traffic implies a reduced chance of getting into an accident, which improves people's safety. Thus, reducing commute time results in both reduced monetary cost and improved road safety.

It is anticipated that future evolutions of ground transportation will ultimately transform into a cyber physical system (CPS). The CPS will be comprised of cyber infrastructure comprised of computers, communication links, and sensor as well as physical infrastructure consisting of roads and vehicles. The cyber infrastructure monitors, controls, and provides decision support for the physical infrastructure. A significant fraction of CPSs have components that are capable of both intelligent communication and control. Added intelligence in the form of sensors, embedded systems, either short- or long-range transceivers, and other computing or communication resources carries the promise of a less invasive operation flow, more robust infrastructure, increased autonomy, and improved safety.

The ground transportation system, however, is considerably more complex than other CPSs such as power grids and water distribution systems. The increased complexity is related to several factors, including:
- both the size and volatility of the underlying databases,
- the number of entities involved (each individual moving object (MO) needs to be accounted for), and
- the human factor involved in the process.

These characteristics are manifested in solutions that address both the frequent update of and efficient access to large data repositories and technical constraints of the cyber infrastructure. The latter issue is not within the scope of this chapter. This chapter discusses both the efficient adaptation of previous techniques and the introduction of new techniques that alleviate the complexity involved in modeling ground transportation systems.

Users access databases by means of queries. The location-based nature of user queries requires the database to answer position-related requests.

Position-related requests are also known as location aware queries (LAQs). For instance, *find the five best restaurants in Chicago* and *find the five best restaurants nearest to my current location* are two LAQs. A closer inspection of the examples reveals a subtle, yet fundamental, difference between the two. The result set of the first query is independent of the location of the user. This is not true with the second query. In another words, the result of the first query will be the same for any issuer regardless of his/her location. For the second query, the result set will vary according to the geographic position of the user. The second query is an example of a location-dependent query (LDQ). LDQs are a subclass of LAQs. Due to dependence on the location of the query issuer, the efficient processing of LDQs is more challenging than other types of LAQs. It becomes more challenging when the queried objects are considered to be moving (eg, *find the five closest taxis to my current location*).

Based on the characteristics of the data and the types of queries, solutions to the aforementioned issues are identified twofold: efficient indexing mechanisms and efficient querying techniques. Indexing is the foundation for supporting queries that target large data sets to achieve both efficiency and accuracy in mobile object-related applications. Most mechanisms for indexing MOs model objects that move freely in Euclidean space [3–5]. Solutions based on Euclidean space are, however, incapable of providing accurate query results under road-network constraints. Introducing these constraints into the mobile object indexing requires development of new indexing schemes to allow more realistic modeling and implementation of MO-related applications. Several recently proposed indexing schemes handled MOs on road networks. These schemes only support queries based on historical or current positions of objects; they do not support predictive queries [6,7]. By means of predictive queries, based on road conditions and route redirection, travelers have the ability to act proactively, improving both efficiency and safety.

In support of such an environment, this chapter discusses and provides solutions to issues of managing and processing mobile data under road-network constrains. This envisioned environment will allow users to travel economically and safely. The solutions comprehend a mobile data indexing structure under the road-network constraints and effective predictive query algorithms.

The remainder of this chapter is organized as follows: Section 2 provides a brief introduction to the representation of ground transportation systems as

CPSs. Section 3 gives an overview of related work on MO indexing. The discussion covers objects moving both on Euclidean space and under road-network constraints. Related work on query processing techniques is discussed in Section 4. Section 5 discusses performance of some recent approaches on predictive query processing that provides traffic information to travelers. Finally, Section 6 concludes the contributions of this chapter and discusses some possible future research expansions.

2. GROUND TRANSPORTATION SYSTEM AS CPS

As noted earlier, the ground transportation system is identified as a CPS. A visual representation of both the cyber and physical components of a typical transportation system is depicted in Fig. 1.

2.1 GTS Infrastructure

The physical components of a ground transportation system are MOs, static objects, and (in most cases) the road network itself (see Fig. 1) [8,9]. MOs are objects capable of movement. They are often referred to as either mobile hosts [10,11] or mobile clients [3,12]. MOs move on a fixed network bound by velocity constraints. Both a person carrying a cellular phone and a vehicle moving on the road are tangible examples of MOs. MOs are usually

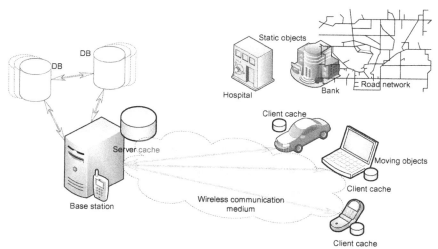

Fig. 1 Moving object infrastructure.

equipped with some type of location-determining device such as a GPS device to sense and measure the speed and position of an MO. SOs are objects with stationary locations such as buildings.

2.2 Infrastructure Representation in CPS

Information on both the road network and the objects is stored at the base station (BS). The road network is represented and stored as a graph $G(E, V)$, where E is the set of edges and V is the set of vertices. Each edge $e \in E$ represents a road segment in the network and $e = v1, v2$, where $v1, v2 \in V$; $v1$ and $v2$ are the starting and ending nodes of the road segment, respectively. An edge could be either a segment that has no intersection [9,13] or a segment that can be represented as a straight line [14]. A vertex on the network represents a point where two segments meet.

Both vertices and edges (ie, segments) are associated with a set of attributes, if available. The edge length and the maximum road speed are two common edge attributes. Information about MOs is stored with respect to the network. For example, a tuple that encapsulates object information would contain identification, current position coordinates, current road segment (ie, an edge in the graph G), next road segment, updated time stamp, and speed.

2.3 Flow of Operations/Requests to Cyber System

Communication between the BS and the MOs occurs wirelessly. Intermediate message support stations, located between BSs and MOs, are used to improve the strength of the communication signal. The information exchanged between the BS and an MO includes the MO's information (sensed by either the MO's GPS or road-side sensors), query requests, and query responses. In a typical application, the user sends the query request to the BS, the BS retrieves the relevant information from a collection of databases, and the result is sent back to the user.

2.4 Location-Dependent Query Taxonomy

A location-dependent query (LDQ) is one of the most demanding query types on mobile object data. It can be classified into several subquery types according to the information it provides (Fig. 2A) or according to their response frequency (Fig. 2B).

Some common types of queries under the information-based query taxonomy include range query (RQ), K nearest neighbor query (KNNQ),

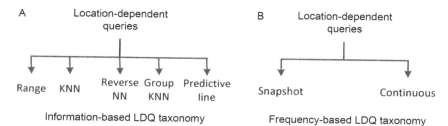

Fig. 2 Location-dependent query taxonomy. (A) Information-based LDQ taxonomy. (B) Frequency-based LDQ taxonomy.

group nearest neighbor query (GNNQ) or sometimes this is referred as aggregated K nearest neighbor query, reverse K nearest neighbor query (RKNNQ), and predictive line query (PLQ).

RQs [4,15,16] search all objects within a user-specified range (eg, "Show me all of the taxis within 10 miles of my current location."). KNNQs [12,15,17–19] provide the K objects nearest to the issuer (eg, "Show me the 5 taxis closest to my current location."). An RKNNQ [20] processes a KNNQ from the object's point of view, not the issuer's (eg, "Show me 5 pedestrians whose nearest taxi driver is me."). The GNNQ [21,22,59] provides a grouped answer to a set of KNNQs (eg, "The best place for n people from different companies/organizations to meet."). In PLQs, a user requires information about either a road segment or the entire route [23] (eg, "What will be the traffic condition of I-44 near Eureka, MO when I get there?").

The information provided by an RQ is similar to that of a KNNQ. The difference comes from both the number of objects in the result set and the area being searched. The RQ restricts the range but relaxes the number of objects the issuer is interested in. The KNNQ is the opposite; it restricts the number of objects but relaxes the range.

Similar to the KNNQ, the RKNNQ also specifies the number of objects to be returned. However, the answers to KNNQ and RKNNQ are not necessarily the same, because KNNQ is from the issuer's perspective, while RKNNQ is from the object's perspective. Consider the aforementioned examples for KNNQ and RKNNQ. In both queries, the taxi driver wants to know about five pedestrians. In the KNNQ example, those five pedestrians are the closest to the issuer. No other pedestrians are closer, but these pedestrians might find some other taxi driver closer to them. KNNQ does not consider the pedestrian's view of the taxi drivers. The RKNNQ, on the other hand, queries for pedestrians who find the issuer within their five closest taxi drivers.

The GNNQ provides an aggregated answer to a set of KNNQs. For example, consider people in n companies/organizations who are trying to schedule a meeting. The best place for everyone to meet may be a site that reduces the total travel time. GNNQ would find a solution to this kind of situation. Thus, the GNNQ response reduces the collective cost metric (such as travel time) to provide an aggregated answer.

Each aforementioned query type can be associated with a time parameter. In such cases, the queries aim to predict object positions at a specific future time stamp. For example, some RQ extensions include predictive time slice queries, window queries, and moving queries. The predictive time slice query (also known as either a future RQ or a predictive RQ) finds all of the MOs that will be inside the query range during the specified future period.

The window query is a generalized form of the time-slice query with coinciding time stamps. The moving query is a further generalization of a window query. The moving query specifies two ranges at two different time stamps: the initial time and the end time. These two ranges could be different in size and/or location. The range at the initial time gradually evolves into the range at the end time. In general, these two ranges can be considered to be one dynamically shaped moving range. The query answer contains all of the MOs that cross the moving range.

Categories of queries under the frequency-based query taxonomy include both snapshot queries and continuous queries. If the query result is provided only once per request then the query is identified as a snapshot query. This query expires when a result is produced. A continuous query processes a request continuously, informing the user of changes in the result set. Continuous queries do not expire with the first response. Instead, requesters may revoke their request when they are no longer interested in the service for that particular query.

The subcategories of these two taxonomies can be corelated as well, eg, snapshot RQs, continuous RQs, snapshot KNNQs, continuous KNNQs, and so on. Queries discussed in the literature are typically snapshot queries.

2.5 Performance Metrics and Challenges

Users expect accuracy, short response times, and information privacy from an LDQ service provider. This chapter focuses on both response time and accuracy. Information privacy is beyond the scope of this work.

The accuracy of a query response can be affected by several parameters including current information, the object's mobility, delays in response, and network constraints. In order for the query response to be accurate it is important for information to be current. However, maintaining up-to-date information is challenging due to the mobility of objects. Each mobile object periodically sends messages to keep its information updated. Assuming an update interval of 120 s, a system with 1 million MOs generates 30 million update messages per hour [18]. The update techniques should be efficient to provide current information at the next query request.

In addition to the impact discussed earlier, the object's mobility also affects the pertinence of the response. Consider the scenario in Fig. 3. Fig. 3A and B shows the snapshots of objects at two time stamps: t_0 and t_1, respectively. An object that issues a KNNQ at point A at time t_1 should receive the response $\{O_6, O_1, O_4\}$ (the solid circles in the figure). However, due to the issuer's mobility the corresponding response might not be received until t_1, when the object has reached point B. At this point, the result is no longer relevant to the user according to his/her current position (see Fig. 3B). This effect will be worse when the response is further delayed. A greater delay result in a greater the deviation from the original position, which will eventually cause it to become obsolete.

An intelligent service provider would consider the mobility of an object and predict its future position at time t_1. It might then generate the result for the issuer at point B accordingly: $\{O_5, O_7, O_8\}$. This information

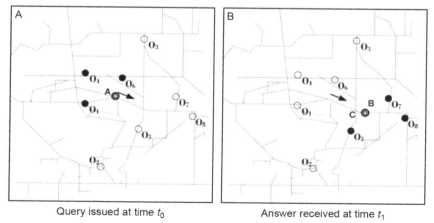

Query issued at time t_0 Answer received at time t_1

Fig. 3 Invalidation of a KNNQ response as time elapse. (A) Query issued at time t_0. (B) Answer received at time t_1.

may be invalid if road network constraints have not been considered. For instance, reaching object O_5 from point B might not be practical from point B when the road network constraints (ie, one-way roads) are considered.

The possible irrelevancy of a response is primarily due to the mobility of objects. Because of the mobility feature, both the information at the database (including both the MO's location and the moving speed) and the query response could become outdated frequently. Efficient update handling techniques address the issues related to keeping the database up to date.

Both enabling fast and accurate responses and taking future behavior of objects into account (supporting predictive information) could abate the issue of out–of-date query response. Providing a fast response from current information is a matter of retrieving relevant information efficiently. Thus, the data collection should be organized and stored in a manner that provides efficient access to relevant data. This leads to the need for efficient data manipulation.

3. INDEXING MOs

Indexing techniques for MO databases have been addressed under two primary categories: indexing objects moving in Euclidean space and indexing objects moving under road-network constraints.

3.1 Indexing MOs in Euclidean Space

Much work has been conducted on indexing MOs in Euclidean space [4,5,24,25]. Most of these approaches model the mobility of objects as a linear function of time, where the position at any given time t, denoted as $x(t)$, can be obtained as defined by (1). Here, x_{ref} represents a reference position at time t_{ref} ($t_{ref} < t$). The velocity vector is represented by v:

$$x(t) = x_{ref} + v(t - t_{ref}) \tag{1}$$

The linear representation of MOs makes predicting an object's future position both simple and constant in time. Hence, fewer update messages are expected from the mobile objects. Fewer update messages, in turn, reduce the update cost. However, the advantage comes at the expense of reduced accuracy.

The indexing structures that utilize linear representation can be classified into several classes depending on their base indexing structure. Some commonly used base structures include the R-tree [26], the B$^+$-tree, and the quadtree [27]. In addition to these structures, some hybrid approaches can also be found in the literature [28].

3.1.1 R-Tree-Based Indexes

R-tree is a height-balanced tree structure. A leaf node of the R-tree maintains the entries for mobile objects. Each object is represented by a tuple (ID, minimum bounding rectangle (MBR)). The ID is the identifier for the object, and the MBR is a rectangle that tightly bounds the object. A nonleaf node of the R-tree maintains all of its children nodes' MBR along with a pointer to each child node.

The time parameterized R-tree (TPR-tree) [4] extends an R*-tree, an improved version of R-tree, by adding velocity information to mobile objects. Each side of the MBR is embedded with a velocity component. Dimensions of the MBR are updated according to these velocities and remain in the updated MBR. The velocities attached on opposite sides of the MBR represent the minimum and the maximum velocity, respectively, along the direction of the moving space.

This velocity information propagates to every MBR up to the root of the tree. Consider Fig. 4A; the gray rectangles (a, b, c, and d) in the figure represent the leaf-node MBRs and the white rectangles (g and h) represent the MBRs of the parents of the leaf nodes. Directions of the leaf nodes are shown

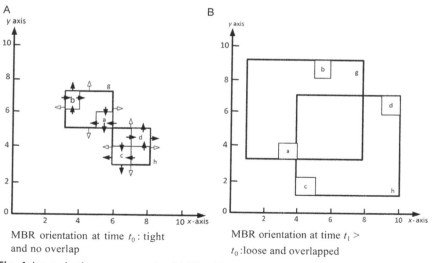

Fig. 4 Issues in time-parameterized MBRs. (A) MBR orientation at time t_0: tight and no overlap. (B) MBR orientation at time $t_1 > t_0$: loose and overlapped.

by the solid arrows attached on each side of the leaf MBR. Each side of a leaf MBR has a velocity magnitude of one. Depending on these velocities (+1 s and −1 s) and the MBRs of their parents, the speed of each side becomes one as well. Directions of parent MBRs are shown by the hollow arrows.

The primary drawback of this approach is the unconditional expansion of MBRs as time elapses. As a result, the MBR may no longer exist and an extensive overlap of MBR could appear. These issues can also be explained with Fig. 4. Recall that a, b, c, and d are leaf nodes, and g and h are their immediate upper level nodes. The velocity magnitude of each of an MBR's edge is one. Fig. 4A and B shows the MBRs at time t_0 (construction time) and time t_1, respectively. As Fig. 4A shows, both leaf node MBRs and parent MBRs represent the MBR at the construction time. At the same time, MBRs do not overlap each other. However, as time evolves, the MBRs both expand extensively and overlap each other. The overlapping of the MBRs increases the search cost [4,5].

Another drawback, specific to the TPR-tree, comes in the design of its maintenance functions (ie, insertion and deletion). These functions are a direct, simple modification of an R*-tree, which was developed for storing static data. Due to this reason, it may be unable to render expected performances for dynamic data indexing in a TPR-tree. The aforementioned behavior mismatch between the indexed objects (mobile) and the supported functions (static) is addressed in the TPR*-tree by improving the insertion and the deletion functions of the TPR-tree.

In the insertion function, when a new node is inserted into the TPR*-tree, the tree travels from the root to the best leaf node that can facilitate the new entry. The subtree is selected according to the lowest value of the predefined penalty metrics (eg, the size of the perimeter and the overlapping area). When two or more subtrees produce the same penalty value, each such subtree is explored further, until one selection becomes dominant. Essentially, every tied subtree is further explored until the best node is reached. This expanded search within a TPR*-tree can result in additional search costs. However, the query performance compensates for this overhead [5]. Research has shown that the overhead associated with obtaining the complete access path (using the proposed approach) is minor [5].

If the selected node is already full, some selected entries will be removed and reinserted into the tree. Doing so reveals other nodes that can facilitate the removed entries while retaining the tree's similar structure (ie, those that contribute to forming the MBR margins are removed). After those are removed, the node's MBR shrinks producing a tighter MBR previously contained the entry. Any overflowed nodes found in the reinsertion process are split. Each of these optimizations introduced into the TPR*-tree led the TPR*-tree to outperform the TPR-tree in terms of query performance [5].

Both the TPR-tree and TPR*-tree suffer from the unconditional expansion of MBRs. This issue was addressed in several later studies [24,25]. Papadopoulos *et al.* [24] proposed handling MOs separately according to their speeds. Saltenis and Jensen [25] introduced an expiration time for function parameters.

The approach proposed by Papadopoulos *et al.* [24] reduces the possibility of having large MBRs; it handles MOs in separate structures according to their speed. Furthermore, Papadopoulos *et al.* [24] handles each dimension of the moving space separately. As a result, this indexing structure needs to maintain several R-tree structures resulting in poor space utilization. More specifically, the space consumption of this approach is almost twice that of a TPR-tree [24]. Determining the proper speed limit is also challenging in this approach.

The indexing technique proposed by Saltenis and Jensen [25] is known as the REXP-tree. This tree embeds an expiration time into the function parameters. Thus, the MBR construction considers the object's life up to the expiration time. The corresponding MBR construction considers this short-term life result in four possible adoptions: always-minimum, conservative, static, and update minimum. The always-minimum strategy ensures that the MBRs tightly bind enclosing objects not only at the construction time but also through the objects' entire lifetime. In this case, each time the object's information deviates from the reported information, the new information is to update the MBRs. Considering all of these changes during the object's lifetime is difficult and impractical to implement; the entire future trajectories of each object must be considered. In conservative MBR construction, a perfect MBR is guaranteed only at construction time. It is not guaranteed subsequently. Static MBR construction defines MBR boundaries by considering both the lower and the upper position limits of the objects for the specified time. An updated-minimum MBR is an improved version of the conservative MBR approach. At each update, the MBR is reconstructed in such a way that velocities of the MBR cover objects with higher speeds up to their expiration time. Regardless of the adoption method, all four MBR construction methods exhibit nearly the same performance characteristics [25].

None of the aforementioned MBR construction approaches remove objects as soon as they expire. Removal requires the tree to be restructured, creating overhead for tree maintenance. Instead, expired objects are removed each time this information is written back from memory to secondary disk. This could result underutilized nodes, as the node capacity is shared by both expired and live entries. Delayed data removal lowers tree maintenance cost at the expense of lower space utilization.

The R-tree with an update memo (RUM-tree) [3] also addresses the restructuring overhead of a tree structure. It handles the update message as an insertion followed by a deletion. The insertion is performed promptly upon receipt of an update message. However, deletion is delayed, which results in multiple versions of objects. These older, unnecessary, versions are removed by a process known as garbage cleaning. Garbage cleaning is activated when the RUM-tree's memory usage is about to overflow. One advantage of these approaches is the transparency of the expired object removal.

In another approach to reduce tree restructuring overhead, Kwon *et al.* [17] proposed the LUR-tree that reviews the possibility of accommodating the new position of an MO within the current MBR. It does so without following the typical update technique (deletion followed by insertion), which can create unnecessary partitioning. Additionally, this method does not require any restructuring of the MBR if the object's new position falls within the current MBR.

If the new object's position falls outside of the current MBR, one of the three following methods is used: traditional deletion and insertion, extension of the MBR, or reinsertion into the parent node. The first method (traditional deletion and insertion) is trivial. The second method (the extension of the MBR) maintains a slightly larger MBR. This expansion is more appropriate for situations in which objects move along the boundary roads in a zigzag motion. In the reinsertion method, the updated object is inserted into the parent node. If the immediate parent node is full, the process propagates up to the root until a suitable candidate is found.

A summary of the aforementioned approaches is presented in Table 1. The summary includes the types of queries, advantages, and drawbacks of each indexing structure discussed earlier.

3.1.2 B^+-Tree-Based Indexes

In general, B^+-tree-based indexing structures convert an object's two-dimensional position to a one-dimensional position. The conversion is performed by means of a space filling curve (eg, either the Hilbert or the Peano curve). In this conversion process, the space is considered as a two-dimensional grid. Every cell in the grid is visited only once. Each cell is then assigned a sequence value. This sequence value is the key used when

Table 1 R-Tree-Based Indexing Schemes for Moving Objects in Euclidean Space

Indexing Name	Supported Queries	Advantages	Drawbacks
TPR-tree [4]	Time slice, window, and moving	Introduce indexing mobile objects in R*-tree	Maintenance functions are not compatible for MO's unconditional expansion problem
TPR*-tree [5]	Window	Improve TPR-tree's maintenance functions of TPR-tree	Unconditional expansion problem
Dual space [24]	Window	Solve unconditional expansion problem and improve the query performance	Poor space utilization (obsolete entries)
R^{EXP}-tree [25]	Time slice, Window	Solve unconditional expansion problem, reduce tree restructuring overhead	Obsolete entries in the tree structure reduce space utilization and query performance
RUM-tree [3]	Range	Reduce tree restructuring overhead	Obsolete entries in the tree structure reduce space utilization and query performance
LUR-tree [17]	Range and KNN	Reduce tree restructuring overhead	MBRs could be not optimal, but bigger. This adds more dead space which will increase the search cost

indexing the objects in a cell in the B^+-tree. Fig. 5 illustrates the assignment of sequence values based on the Peano space-filling curve. The number in each cell represents the sequence number of that particular cell.

The indexing structures proposed in Refs. [12,18,19] have employed both B^+-trees and the aforementioned space filling concept. Technically, these structures are comprised of multiple B^+-trees. One tree is used to maintain the object information within one update interval, while another B^+-tree is used for the subsequent update interval. Maintaining separate B^+-trees provides the index structure with adequate time to clean up all of the object information at the first update interval. The second tree allows for handling the messages within a succeeding update interval. B^+-trees are then used interchangeably.

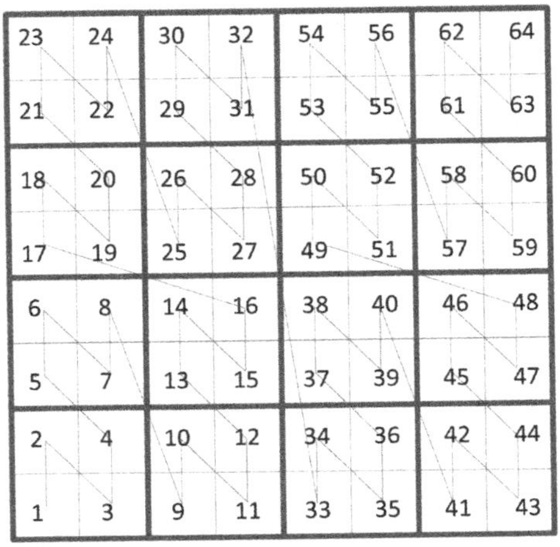

23	24	30	32	54	56	62	64
21	22	29	31	53	55	61	63
18	20	26	28	50	52	58	60
17	19	25	27	49	51	57	59
6	8	14	16	38	40	46	48
5	7	13	15	37	39	45	47
2	4	10	12	34	36	42	44
1	3	9	11	33	35	41	43

Fig. 5 An example of space-filling curve: Peano curve.

The B^x-tree [18] considers the global maximum speed when handling the objects' speeds. This global speed consideration demotes the performance of the B^x-tree, because query results would contain many false positives. The B^{dual}-tree [19] addresses this issue, by considering both the location and speed of an object using a four-dimensional space-filling curve.

Both the B^x-tree and the B^{dual}-tree consider a normal distribution of objects in the Euclidean space. They are unable to perform well on skewed data distribution. Later studies tried to overcome the drawback of B^x-tree sensitivity to skewed data. The ST^2B-tree improves the B^x-tree index to support skewed distribution of objects [12]. Another study [29] kept the index unchanged and improved the query algorithm.

The structures, based on the B^+-tree, are summarized in Table 2.

3.1.3 Quad-Tree-Based Indexes

Different versions of quadtrees are available depending on the type of data supported by the data structure.[a] Some commonly used quadtree types include the PR and the PMR quadtree. An example of a PR quadtree space partition and tree construction is illustrated in Fig. 6.

The PR bucket quadtree is often chosen over an R-tree to avoid the object's MBR representation. Cells are recursively divided into fourths until each cell capacity is less than the tree node capacity. Since the construction process repeatedly divides the space into four-quads tree nodes cannot

---

[a] 2A detailed study of quadtrees and its versions are presented in Ref. [27].

Table 2 R-Tree-Based Indexing Schemes for Moving Objects in Euclidean Space

Indexing Name	Supported Queries	Advantages	Drawbacks
B^x-tree [18]	Range, KNN, continuous range and KNN	Solve unconditional expansion problem	Use global speed Sensitive for skewed data
B^{dual}-tree [19]	Range and KNN	Solve global speed consideration problem	Sensitive for skewed data
ST^2B-tree [12]	Range and KNN	Address he sensitiveness in the skewed data	Self-tunability requires additional online processing and storage

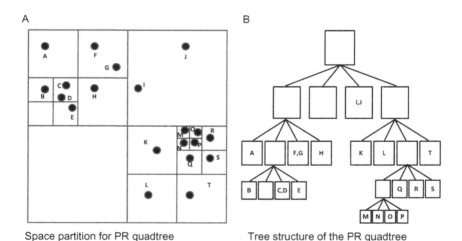

Space partition for PR quadtree   Tree structure of the PR quadtree

Fig. 6 An example of PR quadtree. (A) Space partition for PR quadtree. (B) Tree structure of the PR quadtree.

overlap. As noted earlier, the quadtree is not required to define MBRs explicitly, but only as points. This point representation is easier to handle than MBRs.

The scalable trajectory index for predicted positions within MO databases (STRIPES) [16] extends the PR bucket quadtree to index mobile objects. STRIPES consider each moving dimension separately, applying a dual transformation for each dimension. The mobility representation of an object is then altered from a line to a point (v, x_{ref}), where v and x_{ref} represent the object's velocity vector and the reference position at time t_{ref} $(t_{ref} < t)$, respectively. These points are stored in a PR bucket quadtree [30].

STRIPES maintains two similar PR bucket quadtree structures for two consecutive time periods. These structures are used interchangeably in future periods, providing enough time for the previously used structure to flush old information while preparing for the next time period. Consequently, the updating object information is completely isolated from the query processing. As a result, the maintenance cost can be neglected, as it is offline.

3.1.4 Hybrid Indexing Structures

The Q+R-tree [28] is a hybrid structure that combines a quadtree with the R*-tree. Each tree is built separately. The quadtree stores fast mobile objects, while the R-tree maintains slow objects. The definitions of both fast and slow objects were primarily based, on the subspace on which they move. For example, parking lots and the areas around homes and offices are considered slow movement regions. These areas can be identified according to either a map or historical data.

In contrast to the traditional R*-tree, the Q+R-tree maintains neither a lower nor an upper bound for the number of objects stored in the leaf node. Instead, it stores all of the objects in one region in one MBR. This is done to reduce both the insertion and the update cost, as two MBRs will not overlap one another. This approach does not use the R*-tree is in a traditional manner, and the literature does not clearly explain the reason for using an R*-tree [28]. The index, however, performs better than either an individual quadtree or the R*-tree.

The Q+R-tree is different from the aforementioned approaches as it does not rely on the linear representation of an MO. Instead, it expects update messages to maintain up-to-date position information.

3.1.5 Summary

This section addressed some recently developed structures that index mobile objects in Euclidean space. Structures were categorized according to their base structure. The most common base structures included the R-tree, the B^+-tree, and the quadtree. In addition to those indexing structures, some hybrid versions of the common base structures were discussed. Their key features and impacts on indexing (within parenthesis) are compared in Table 3.

A comparative analysis of these approaches is difficult due to differences between the inconsistency of the experimental environments and the lack of a common benchmark. The experimental study conducted by Chen

Table 3 A Comparison of Different Base Structures as Moving Object Indexing structures in Euclidean Space

Feature	R-Tree	B⁺-tree	B⁺-tree
Space partition	Dynamic (handling space upgrades/degrades are easy) overlapped subspaces are possible (high search cost) dynamic, height balance tree (high restructuring cost)	Static (handling space upgrades/degrades needs redesign) no overlaps (less search cost)	Dynamic (handling space upgrades/degrades are easy) no overlaps (less search cost)
Tree structure	Dynamic, height balance tree (high restructuring cost)	Static, height balance tree (less restructuring cost)	Dynamic, height balance tree (high restructuring cost)
MO representation	Velocities and attached to MBRs (introduces unconditional MBR expansion problem, but easy to simulate the mobility)	Objects 2D position is Converted into a 1D sequence number (add extra processing overhead to updates and query execution)	Dynamic (handling update messages usually demands tree restructuring)

et al. [31], however, compared the performance of several of the aforementioned index structures. This study includes the TPR-tree, the TPR*-tree, the RUM-tree, the STRIPES, the B^x-tree, and the B^{dual}. Among these, the B^+-tree-based indexes (ie, the B^x- and the B^{dual}-tree) demonstrated the best update performance with a reasonable query cost. Both the TPR- and the TPR*-trees gave the best query performances at the expense of the worst update performance. With regard to storage, the TPR-tree and the TPR*-tree consumed the least amount of storage. Both the B^x-tree and the B^{dual}-tree consumed storage close to that of the TPR- and TPR*-trees.

Chen *et al.* [31] concluded that the TPR-tree is better for an environment that requires a greater number of queries with fewer updates. This conclusion was further extended to include two more environments: environments that require fewer queries and higher updates and environments whose behavior is unknown. It was shown that the B^x-tree is better in the former environment, while STRIPES is superior for an unknown environment [31].

The Euclidean space mobility representation is mostly suitable when the objects have random moving behavior (eg, animals and mobile sensors). However, random movement is not practical for all types of objects. For example, vehicles are confined to the underlying road networks. Thus, these indexes might not be able to effectively support mobile object indexing under road-network constraints.

3.2 Indexing MOs on Road Network

Knowing that object mobility is constrained to an underlying infrastructure allows a server to provide more precise information to mobile users [13,32,33]. The road network constraint, however, invalidates the mobility patterns assumed in the Euclidean space and their approaches.

Research based on Euclidean space mobility patterns is mainly based on two primary assumptions: the linear movements and constant/random speeds of mobile objects. The linear movement can no longer be accepted, as the roads cannot be assumed to be straight lines. Instead, these mobile objects move along paths through the road network where more direction changes can exist. At the same time, the speed may be neither steady nor random. Rather, the mobile objects might change speeds depending on speed limits, weather condition, road condition, and so forth.

Mobile object indexing under road network constraints has been addressed under two categories: historical positions of MOs [34–36] and real-time positions of MOs [9,21,37]. The latter category will be discussed in detail in the following sections while the former category is out of the scope of this chapter.

The general approach when handling real-time objects under road-network constraints involves indexing the objects' information with respect to the road network (known as composite structures) [9,21,23,37]. Composite structures use spatial indexing methods (ie, an R-tree, an R*-tree, and a PMR quadtree), grids, tables, and/or hash tables with reference to the corresponding road segments to store the information about road network and the MOs, respectively. The general idea of a composite structure is illustrated in Fig. 7. As the figure depicts, the triangle represents the road network indexing structure.

This structure is usually arranged as a hierarchical tree structure. The leaf level of the tree points to the road segments. The mobile object information is stored under these road segments.

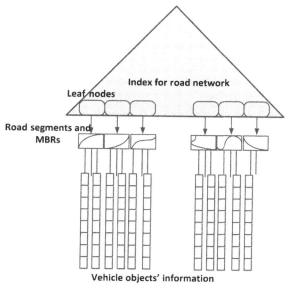

Fig. 7 An example of composite structure.

The road network is indexed in R-tree family indexes (eg, either R-tree or R*-tree). When an object travels from road segment to another, it is removed from the current road segment and stored under the new road segment. There are two main drawbacks to this indexing. First, a significant amount of dead space exists in a road segment's MBR. The dead space is the redundant space within the MBR but outside the road segment. This redundancy can lead to false overlaps of MBRs that, in turn, increases the search cost. The second drawback is due to the mandatory search cost involved in maintaining update messages. MBRs do not capture road segment connectivity. Thus, to locate the next road segment that the object is going to move to, the tree must be searched. To resolve this issue, Bok *et al.* [6] and Feng *et al.* [7] proposed two separate (but similar) techniques in order to capture the road network connectivity. Bok *et al.* [6] proposed the intersection–oriented network R-tree (INOR-tree). The premise is to store multiple edges connected to the same intersection in the same MBR. By doing so, some object updates can be done within the same MBR when the objects travel from one edge to another. Feng *et al.* [7] suggested storing a fraction of each contributing edge to form a junction in the MBR. This indexing structure is known as a cross region (CR)-tree. The primary difference between the INOR-tree and the CR-tree is that the CR-tree maintains the fraction of the edge, whereas the INOR-tree defines new junctions where the edge is split by the MBR margin. However, because the CR-tree stores both the edge and its corresponding fraction, edges are duplicated if they are covered by multiple MBRs. This duplication leads to reduced space utilization.

Nevertheless, for a particular road map with the exact same MBRs, both methods consume approximately the same amount of storage. The INOR-tree stores an edge several times, while the CR-tree splits an edge into a number of subedges and stores them separately. If the number of repeated edges and the number of splits are equal, the amount of space required in both methods is approximately the same.

One disadvantage of the CR-tree and the INOR-tree is that modifying the road network adversely impacts the index structure. Both methods are equally complex when compared to single road-segment-based indexing (ie, determining the proper road segment units, finding the MBR, and so forth). This complexity might be one reason that these novel indexing schemes have not been explored extensively.

The single edge storage unit, however, has been used in many composite structures. These structures can be classified into several categories depending on their storage method: disk-based, memory-based, and hybrid-based indexing schemes.

Disk-based indexing schemes consider both network and vehicle information stored in the secondary disk. Thus, their primary performance metric is the required number of page accesses. One primary advantage of disk-based index structures is higher scalability. However, these index structures might not handle updates efficiently due to the communication delays associated with access to the secondary storage.

Memory-based indexing structures store information in memory. Their common performance metric is CPU time. Since memory access is faster than disk access, query processing and vehicles update handling are faster with these approaches than disk-based approaches. However, they typically show low scalability as the memory space is limited.

The hybrid-based indexing structures utilize both secondary disk and memory to store information (hence both page accesses and CPU time can be employed to report performance). Most of the time, the secondary storage maintains road network information, while memory maintains the vehicle information. The hybrid-based approaches that utilize memory to maintain the vehicle information also update this information faster (similar to the memory-based approaches). Additionally, these approaches might be scalable on the network size but not the amount of vehicles in the network.

3.2.1 Disk-Based Indexes

Some of the disk-based composite structures include IMORS (indexing moving objects on road sectors) [32], the adaptive network R-tree (ANR-tree) [13], the R-TPR±-tree [21], R^D-tree [23], and the TPR^{uv} [38]. Each of these structures uses an R-tree-like structure with leaf nodes that point to road segments. Each indexing scheme has demonstrated the ability to support different queries: range [32], predictive range [13], predictive traffic flow [21,23], and continuous queries [38].

IMORS [32] stores road information using an R*-tree. A leaf node of the tree points to a list of mobile objects that are moving on a road segment (the road sector block). IMORS uses a separate data block to maintain the mobile objects' information including the position coordinates and velocity. Each entry in the data block is bidirectionally connected to the corresponding object information in the road sector block. This allows the user to locate the corresponding road segment information from the object information and vice versa.

The ANR-tree [13] is comprised of both an R-tree and an in-memory direct access table. The R-tree stores segments of the road network. Leaf nodes in an ANR-tree, similar to IMORS, also maintain the information for MOs on the corresponding road segment. Additionally, the ANR-tree introduces a grouping concept, known as adaptive units (AUs), for the objects within a road segment. An AU group objects with similar moving patterns. This similarity is defined according to the direction of travel along the road segment, a speed threshold and a distance threshold. One road segment could have several AUs, depending on the presence of different moving patterns. Each AU maintains trajectory bounds, which capture the entry time to and predicted exit time from (the trajectory bounds) the segment. These times will be used during the query process. The direct access table of a segment contains the number of objects stored, the trajectory bounds, and a pointer to each AU disk page.

The R-TPR±-tree [21] has also applied concepts similar to the ANR-tree. For example, the R-TPR±-tree uses an R-tree for storage. It also considers similar mobility patterns of objects. The similar patterns in the R-TPR±-tree, however, are defined only by the direction in which they are moving along the road segment.

In addition to the R-tree, the R-TPR±-tree [21] maintains a set of TPR±-trees. These TPR±-trees are attached to the leaf nodes of the

R-tree. Each tree maintains the objects moving on the corresponding road segment. The root of the TPR±-tree points to two child TPR-trees; each represents objects that are moving in the same direction. With this structure, the R-TPR±-tree [21] tries to reduce the expansion of MBRs by separating the objects according to their moving direction. Thus, the expansion of the MBR boundaries is not as severe as it was with the TPR-trees. However, a considerable number of mobile objects must be present on the road segment to realize the advantage of TPR-tree adoption over other list-based structures such as the direct access table in the ANR-tree. Furthermore, it might not perform well for road networks with shorter road segments.

The TPR^{uv}-tree [38] is comprised of an R-tree, a direct access table, and adjacent lists. Similar to the indexes previously discussed, the R-tree indexes road network information. A direct access table is connected for each leaf node in an R-tree. Each entry in this table maintains information regarding that particular road segment. This information includes the road ID, the speed limit, adjacent lists for each end node, and a pointer to the mobile objects. The indexing structure handles update messages through the adjacent lists. The TPR^{uv}-tree provides an almost constant time update cost [38].

The R^{D}-tree consists of an R*-tree [39] and a set of hash tables. R*-tree's leaf nodes also point to hash tables that represent the MOs on each road segment. Each hash table has N hash buckets (a system parameter), and each hash bucket has two sorted lists that provide finer grouping for objects. Objects moving with similar traveling directions are hashed to the same hash bucket. The reason for doing so is based on the observation that two objects moving closer to each other and toward the same geographical destination are likely to have either similar (or the same) travel path because drivers tend to take the shortest path. The traveling direction is determined by the angle between a horizontal line and the line connecting the object's current position to its destination. In Fig. 8, object O's traveling

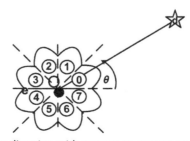

Fig. 8 Object's traveling direction with respect to current road segment.

direction is indicated by θ and hence falls into the hash bucket 0 (where $N=8$). Formally, an object's hash value $H(O)$ is: $[\theta/(360/N)]$. An object's corresponding list index within the hash bucket is again based on its traveling direction. In fact, the area corresponding to a hash bucket is divided into halves, and each half is coupled with a linked list. The list index is determined based on the traveling direction's overlap on the subarea as follows:

$$\begin{cases} 0 & \text{if } 0 \leq \theta - \left\lfloor \dfrac{360 - H(O)}{N} \right\rfloor \leq \dfrac{360}{2N} \\ 1 & \text{if } \dfrac{360}{2-N} \leq \theta - \left\lfloor \dfrac{360 - H(O)}{N} \right\rfloor \leq \dfrac{360}{N} \end{cases}$$

The group update time parameter R-tree (GTR) [40] and the robust GTR (RGTR) [41] are index structures that support efficient updates through group-wise execution. Both insertion and deletion messages are buffered and performed in groups. They neglect the updates sent by vehicles with constant velocities. The user, however, is required to send previous velocity information in update messages to determine the velocity's steadiness. Thus, these models increase the communication cost when compared to a traditional update message environment. The difference between GTR and RGTR appears in their data structures. The RGTR discards the buffer that was keeping track of update messages in the GTR. Instead, updates are performed instantly, as an insertion followed by a deletion. The additional cost is traded off by introducing compressed object representation, which allows tree nodes to accommodate more objects.

A tabulated summary of the disk-based indexing schemes is presented in Table 4.

3.2.2 Memory-Based Indexes

One common approach to improve update costs includes memory-employed indexes [9,37,42,43] and hybrid indexes [15,44], which also utilize memory will be covered in Section 3.2.3). Memory-employed indexes, usually, employ lists [9,42] or tables [37,43] to maintain information about mobile objects. The road network could be indexed as either an R-tree [43] or a PMR quadtree [9,37].

Implementation of the R-tree family index in memory is similar to that of disk-based indexes. The PMR quadtree, however, organizes the entire space into a PMR quadtree. A leaf of the tree contains the covered edge IDs. Connectivity among the edges is maintained in a table.

The aforementioned memory-based indexing structures are compared each other in Table 5.

Table 4 Secondary Disk-Based Indexing Schemes for Moving Objects Under Fixed Network

Indexing Name	Road Network	Mobile Objects	Supported Queries	Continuity	Predictivity
IMORS [32]	R*-tree	Data blocks for each R-tree leaf node	Range	Snapshot	Current
ANR-tree [8]	R-tree	Adaptive unit(s) for each R-tree leaf node.	Range	Snapshot	Predictive
R-TPR±-tree [21]	R-tree	TPR±-tree for each R-tree leaf	Navigation	Snapshot	Predictive
TPR^{uv} [38]	Both an R-tree and adjacent lists	Direct access table	KNN	Continuous	Current
GTR [40]	R-tree	Object list for each leaf node of an R-tree	Range	Snapshot	Current
RGTR [41]	R-tree	Object list for each leaf node of an R-tree	Range	Snapshot	Current
R^D-tree [23]	R*-tree	Hash table for each R-tree leaf node; separate hash bucket depending on the objects geographical direction group	Line	Snapshot and continuous	Current and predict

3.2.3 Hybrid-Based Indexes

Hybrid approaches typically store road network information on the secondary disk, while the mobile objects are maintained in memory (eg, MOVing objects in road network (MOVNet) [15]). The MOVNets employ both an R*-tree to store static road network information and an in-memory grid structure to store object positions. The grid structure divides the entire mobile area into cells. Each cell maintains a list of mobile objects whose

Table 5 Memory-Based Indexing Schemes for Moving Objects Under Fixed Network

Indexing Name	Road Network	Mobile Objects	Supported Queries	Continuity	Predictivity
SR*-tree [42]	Both an R*-tree and a table	Object list	Range	Continuous	Current
DLM [9]	PMR quad	List	Reverse KNN	Continuous	Predictive
Prediction distance table [43]	B⁺-tree	Hash table (on destination)	Range	Snapshot	Predictive
SI and ET [37]	A PMR quadtree	A hash table on the edge id (ET)	NN	Continuous	Current

current location falls into that cell. Updates from mobile objects are directly handled in the grid cells. The R*-tree is accessed whenever the road network distance is required. For example, in a query process, the corresponding Euclidean space query is performed on the grid first. The R*-tree is then searched to obtain the corresponding road segments. Finally, a partial map is constructed in memory to consider the network's distance.

Disposable index for moving objects (DIME) [44] focuses on reducing update costs. DIME manages several indexing structures, both in secondary disk and in memory, to maintain an object's position. When the objects on secondary disks must be updated, a new in-memory index is created. This index maintains only the objects whose positions were updated. Entries in the initial on-disk tree structures are not updated with the new location information. Instead, they are flagged as obsolete. When the in-memory entries receive position-updates, another new index is created to maintain them. Essentially, no indexing structure is modified for an update message; a new index is created instead and the old indexes are disposed.

There are several drawbacks to this method. One is that all objects' positions may eventually be placed in memory, although DIME begins with a secondary disk index structure. A lower update cost will be penalized at query processing as both the obsolete and valid entries are filtered out at that time.

A summary of hybrid-based indexing schemes are presented in Table 6.

Table 6 Hybrid-Based Indexing Schemes for Moving Objects Under Fixed Network

Indexing Name	Road Network	Mobile Objects	Supported Queries	Continuity	Predictivity
MOVNet [15]	R*-tree (disk)	Array of objects (in memory)	KNN and Range	Snapshot, continuous	Current
DLME[44]	—	Either R*-tree or B$^+$-tree (both in memory and disk)	Range	Continuous	Current

4. QUERY PROCESSING

This section first discusses query algorithms for major types of location-dependent queries based on the information they provide, including RQ, KNNQ, and PLQ. Then, it discusses differences between snapshot queries and continuous queries.

These queries have been studied under Euclidean space and under road-network constraints. When the queries are considered under road-network constraints, distance measurements in the query process are considered in terms of network distance. This consideration is more realistic than considering Euclidean space distances. Hence, this section limits the discussion only to the work that considers the road-network constraints.

4.1 Information-Based Queries

4.1.1 Range Query

RQ searches and retrieves all of the objects within a user-defined range. The query can be formally defined as follows:

Definition 1. Range Query

Given a set of objects O, a query point q and a distance d, RQ of q is the set of objects S, $S \subset O$, where for any $s_i \in S$, the dist(s_i, q) $\leq d$ and dist(a,b) is the network distance between a and b.

The common procedure for processing an RQ under the road-network constraints is comprised of two basic steps [15,32,40,41]. The first step processes a Euclidean space RQ (see Fig. 9) with the same query parameters (ie, the query point and the query range). Fig. 9 visually illustrates a Euclidean space RQ. Here the query point is at the center and the query range is a circle. The Euclidean space RQ retrieves all of the road segments within the

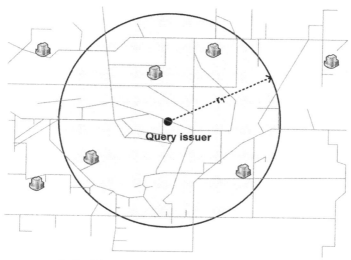

Fig. 9 Range query in Euclidean space.

specified range. The second step considers network distances of objects that are moving on the selected road segments.

The aforementioned process is changed when the issuer requests a predictive query, such as a predictive RQ. In a predictive RQ the issuer requests object information within a specific range for a specific future time. For example, objects that will be in the rectangular region (x_1, y_1, x_2, y_2) during the time interval (T_1, T_2), where (x_1, y_1) is the coordinate of the bottom left-hand corner of the region, and (x_2, y_2) is the coordinate of the top right-hand corner of the region [8]. The predictive RQ process first retrieves road segments in the query range. These road segments cover the objects in the query's specific range, but at the current time. To retrieve the objects at the future time, the road segments are expanded to adjacent road segments. Individual objects on those road segments are examined to determine which objects will enter the query range at the query time.

4.1.2 K Nearest Neighbor Query

KNNQ provides the K objects nearest to the issuer. The query is formally defined as follows:

Definition 2. K Nearest Neighbor Query

Given a set of objects O and a query point q, KNN of q is the set of objects S, $S \subset O$, where for all $s_i \in S$ and $s_j \in (O-S)$, the dist$(s_i, q) \leq$ dist(s_j, q), $i \leq K$, and dist(a,b) is the network distance between a and b.

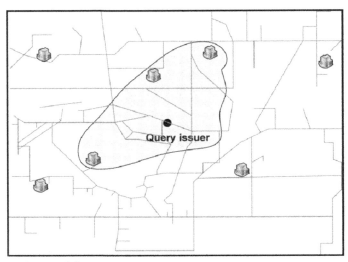

Fig. 10 KNNQ in Euclidean space.

KNNQ processing differs from RQ processing since the upper bound for the range size is unknown. Fig. 10 gives a visual illustration of the KNNQ's search area and its result. For this reason, the most common method for processing KNNQs is incremental search, starting from the query point until K objects are found [15].

The KNNQ algorithm proposed in Ref. [15] is supported by a grid structure. Each grid cell maintains only the number of objects covered by the cell. This method first traverses the grid structure while counting the number of vehicles covered by cells. As soon as K objects are counted, the maximum Euclidean distance is reported. The corresponding road segments are then loaded from the R-tree to form a partial graph. Next, each connected road segment is traversed, starting from the query point. In this traversal, the road distances are considered. The distance calculation which is an online calculation increases the query processing time. To reduce the online processing time, some approaches have considered off-line network computation. The off-line distance computation, however, consumes more storage than the online processing method.

4.1.3 Predictive Line Query
The PLQ allows a user to query the traffic conditions of a specific road segment. The query returns predicted traffic condition of the specified road

segment at the time that the user is expected to travel that segment. Its formal definition is as follows:

Definition 3. Predictive Line Query

A PLQ $= (e_q; t_q; t_c)$ retrieves all MOs which will be on the query road segment e_q at the query time t_q, where $t_q > t_c$ and tc is query issuing time. Ring query RQ $= (e_q; r_1; r_2)$ retrieves MOs whose current locations are in the ring defined by the concentric circles with the midpoint of the query road segment e_q as center and r_1 and r_2 as radius, where $r_1 = v_{min} (t_q - t_c)$ and $r_2 = v_{max} (t_q - t_c)$ [23].

The work presented in Ref. [23] proposed three heuristic-based query algorithms for PLQ processing. Each algorithm is comprised of two basic phases: filtering and refinement phase. The filtering phase extracts the objects that have potential to enter the queried road segment. Its first step is to retrieve the road segments that potential vehicles are travelling on using a ring shaped query as shown in Fig. 11. The ring's outer and inner radii represent the furthest and the closest potential vehicle's current position, respectively. Next, the vehicles moving on those road segments are retrieved. This step is varied in three algorithms. One algorithm, the basic algorithm, selects objects from up to two hash buckets, where each bucket has two linked lists of objects. Another algorithm, named enhanced algorithm, also maintains these lists, but the objects are ordered

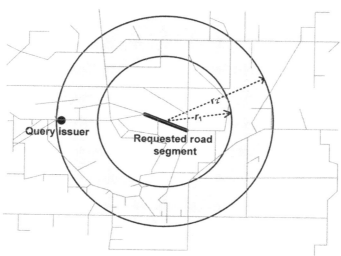

Fig. 11 The initial filtering with a ring query.

(in decreasing order) according to the distance to their destinations. The search terminates at the point where the destination is earlier than the queried road segment. The third algorithm, the comprehensive algorithm, guarantees exactly two lists are accessed.

The query proposed by Feng et al. [21] is similar to PLQ. In fact, they proposed a snapshot query algorithm to obtain predicted traffic flow within a given range (ie, multiple road segments). The algorithm retrieves all road segments within the query range (a circular range as shown in Fig. 9) and considers all objects in a road segment as a group instead of examining individual objects to confirm their presence in the query range. This group-wise comparison requires fewer page accesses at the expense of lower accuracy [21].

These two approaches were compared in Ref. [23] and the results show that all three algorithms in Ref. [23] performs better than Feng's algorithm [21]; the ring query in the filtering phase is one contributing factor for the performance improvement.

Aforementioned snapshot queries are summarized in Table 7.

Table 7 Snapshot Queries under Fixed Network

Query Algorithm	Query Types	Advantages and Disadvantages
Prabhakar et al. [45]	Range	Introduces the indexing queries instead of objects, safe regions reduces the update cost
Cai et al. [46]	Range	Distributed workload among clients gives scale up at server
Cai et al. [47]	Range	Improves [46] to supports heterogeneity of clients, clients work load is not uniform
Hu et al. [48]	Range and KNN	Safe region reduces communication cost, higher client privacy preserving, grouping queries on cell basis reduces the unnecessary query consideration and hence provides the scalability.
Wang and Zimmermann [14]	Range	Less execution cost, higher storage cost due to obsolete entries
Mouratidis et al. [49]	KNN	Less work load at the client

4.2 Frequency-Based Queries

4.2.1 Snapshot Queries

A snapshot query provides a query result only once, and the query expires once the result is produced. The querying techniques discussed in the previous section fall under the snapshot query category.

4.2.2 Continuous Queries

The term *continuous* refers to the continuous monitoring of an issued query. This continuity can come in one of two forms: the continuous monitoring of a static query and the continuous monitoring of a dynamic query (often known as moving queries). Static queries have parameters that do not change over time (eg, the value of K or the issuer's position in KNNQs). However, the query result might be changed when the querying objects move. Dynamic queries refer to the queries whose parameters might change over time. In either case, frequent or large number of update messages should be handled in an efficient manner to produce up-to-date query results.

Regardless of the query category, a naive approach to answering a continuous query involves recalculating the same snapshot query at every timestamp until the query expires. This process may involve a great deal of wasted effort if the query results at consecutive timestamps do not change. The query results need to be updated only when an object in the current result becomes invalid or a new object joins the result due to a change in previously considered information.

Most approaches to continuous queries process queries in two main phases: an initial phase and a maintenance phase. The initial phase generates results for new queries. The maintenance phase maintains the results obtained in the initial phase while considering the influence of the mobility of objects on the query result.

Evaluating each received update message is the simplest method to identify the influenced mobile objects. However, this evaluation could directly affect performance by increasing both processing and communication costs. Thus, the research has focused on efficient query processing techniques to reduce these costs.

One technique commonly used to handle high-frequency update messages involves defining safe regions for MOs. Here the movement of objects within the safe region does not alter the result. The safe region could be calculated and managed by either the object itself, the server, or both [46–48]. If the safe regions are known to the object, the object initiates an update message when the object exits the safe region. In some situations, the update message itself cannot confirm the alteration of the query result(s). When this occurs, the server probes the object information selectively.

Details of the aforementioned techniques can be different for static and dynamic queries. Thus, the details of continuous query processing techniques discussed in previous studies will be addressed separately here. These techniques focus on handling not only the mobile object updates, as well as the data structures used to maintain both queries and query results.

4.2.2.1 Continuous Monitoring on Static Queries

Prabhakar et al. [45] proposed an approach that supports static range queries on mobile objects whose movements are relaxed for Euclidean space. This study did not consider object indexing. Instead, it used query indexing (QI). As a result, every query is indexed in an R-tree-based structure known as QI.

The initial query response is obtained by searching overlapped queries (from the QI) against the position of each object. Once the initial result is obtained, the maintenance phase compares only the object's update messages with the QI. The QI indexes these queries according to their spatial closeness, so each update message is compared against the QI. This process scales up with the number of queries. However, it does not scale up to the higher number of objects.

An individual object maintains its own safe region, calculated by the server, to reduce the number of update messages. The safe region is calculated as the shortest distance between the object and a query boundary. This calculation method has several drawbacks. First, the advantage of keeping track of a safe region decreases when the safe region is small (ie, a dense environment). Objects in smaller the safe regions have a higher chance of crossing the safe region. This leads to sending frequent update messages. Second, the safe regions must be reevaluated each time a query expires or a new query is received, which increases the safe-region maintenance cost.

Another approach [22], which addresses the continuous version of PLQ (CPLQ), also maintains query information in a separate data structure named TPR^Q-tree. The base structure of the TPR^Q-tree is an R*-tree (Fig. 12). The tree allows for group-wise analysis of update messages. The tree indexes an *influence region* (IR) for each PLQ. The influence region is the region that covers a majority of the MOs that may enter the queried road segment at the

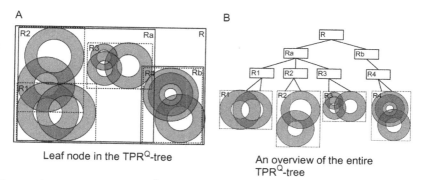

Fig. 12 The structure of the TPR^Q-tree. (A) Leaf node in the TPR^Q-tree. (B) An overview of the entire TPR^Q-tree.

specified future time. The update messages from vehicles in this area will be considered to identify possible changes to the query result. An IR is represented as the parameterized ring which has moving speed attached to both the inner and outer radius. The inner radius is associated with a minimum moving speed toward the queried road segment, while the outer radius is associated with a maximum speed toward the queried road segment.

The CPLQ algorithm consists of two phases: the initial phase and the maintenance phase. The initial phase computes the query result that is valid at the query issuing time. It first searches the TPR^Q-tree to find similar, previously issued queries. If a similar query cannot be found in the TPR^Q-tree, the new query is inserted into the tree and the snapshot PLQ process is applied [23]. The maintenance phase maintains the query results as time passes. Upon receiving an update message from a vehicle, the server checks whether the update affects existing queries by comparing the update message with the influence ranges stored in the TPR^Q-tree. If the existing queries are affected, the changes are reported to the user. To identify the queries affected by the update messages, the authors [22] propose three query maintenance algorithms: solo-update (SU) maintenance, solo-object (SO) maintenance, and batch-object (BO) maintenance algorithm. The algorithms search the TPR^Q-tree for two sets of CPLQs: the set containing the object at its previous update timestamp (denoted as Q_{old}) and the set containing the object after its update at the current timestamp (denoted as Q_{new}).

The SU maintenance algorithm considers the update of object information as two parts separately and finds Q_{old} and Q_{new} separately. Since they are two consecutive points on an object's path, the old and new positions of an object found in the same update messages are usually close together. Therefore, the new and old positions in an object's single update message are very likely to be covered by the influence regions of the same or nearby CPL queries. Based on this observation, the SO maintenance algorithm searches for both the Q_{new} and Q_{old} simultaneously in one round of the search in the TPR^Q-tree. The BO algorithm, on the other hand, considers group-wise update comparison against the TPR^Q-tree. The reason is that it is likely that some update messages are from nearby objects and may influence the same or nearby CPL queries. Thus, upon receiving the update messages at a timestamp, the BO algorithm conducts two rounds of grouping: (i) based on their old update timestamps and (ii) based on their location proximity. The groups are compared against TPR^Q-tree to find Q_{new} and Q_{old}. The BO algorithm shows the best performance among the tree algorithms and SO shows the second best performance.

Cai et al. [46,47] also addressed the static continuous RQ. This study proposed two methods: spatial query management (SQM) [46] and monitoring query management (MQM) [47]. The difference between these two methods is found in the mobile objects' computational capability. Mobile objects considered under MQM are heterogeneous, whereas they are homogeneous when considered in SQM.

In each of these approaches the entire space is divided into disjoint subspaces known as subdomains. The safe region is defined in terms of these subdomains. An object's safe region, in the MQM, is comprised of one or more subdomains. The number of subdomains is decided according to the object's computational capability. In contrast, in the SQM, each object is assigned to only one subdomain. Calculating this safe region is significantly simpler when compared to that of QI [45].

A binary partition tree (BP-tree) maintains a list of overlapped safe regions known as monitoring regions. Mapping between the monitoring region and the query is maintained in a relevance table. The initial phase of a continuous query execution is performed on the BP-tree. The query region of the newly issued query is compared with that of the BP-tree to calculate the monitoring regions. The objects in the relevant subdomains are then informed based on these monitoring regions.

The maintenance phase is primarily handled by the query candidates. These candidates report their influence on the query result. The server then updates the query issuer according to these reports. Thus, the workload at the server is much less when compared to the query process in Ref. [45]. As the computational workload is distributed among the mobile objects, this method scales well with large number of queries and large number of MOs.

The approach proposed by Hu *et al.* [48] also considers safe regions to reduce communication costs. The primary difference between this approach and the aforementioned approaches is that this approach does not index an object's actual position instead; it indexes the safe regions for each object.

The query information and their results are maintained in a memory query index. The query index is constructed in a manner similar to that of the BP-tree [46,47]; the entire space is partitioned into a grid of disjoint areas. The cells (known as quarantine areas) are indexed in the query index. Each cell points to the information about query regions partially overlapped with the cell similar to the monitoring region in Refs. [46,47].

An object's safe region for one specific query is either the quarantine area or its complement, depending on whether or not the object is in the quarantine area. An object's overall safe region is the intersection of the individual query-safe regions.

The experimental results suggest that the approach proposed in Ref. [48] is scalable to the number of registered queries. This scalability has been achieved since the pointer in a grid cell points to all of the queries whose quarantine areas overlap with the cell. Hence, only the relevant queries will be examined.

Wang and Zimmermann [14] proposed algorithms for a continuous RQ by extending the indexing structure they proposed for MOVNet [15]. Within these proposed algorithms, each cell in the grid maintains a list of vertices that connect to other cells. The distance between each connected node pair within the cell is also maintained in addition to the information maintained in MOVNet.

Once an RQ is issued, the edges relevant to the issuer's cell are retrieved from the secondary disk. The shortest distance-based tree (SD-tree) is created from these edges, with the query point as the root. Paths between nodes in the tree provide the shortest distance among them. When the query issuer moves, the tree is rotated. This rotation requires the tree to expand along the subtree to which the query pointer moves. It also requires the other subtrees to be trimmed. When other vehicles move, the new position is compared against the SD-tree and either added or removed to/from the tree and the previous query result is updated accordingly. The primary drawback to this approach is the amount of data managed in memory; only the road network is stored on secondary disk. The information about the vehicles, connectivity, and the SD-tree is stored in main memory. This becomes worse when the number of queries in one cell increases. At that point, each query needs to maintain an SD-tree.

Mouratidis *et al.* [49] proposed a method to process continuous queries for nearest neighbors. In this method, the safe region is a circle whose radius is the distance to NN. The service area is considered a grid. The process begins at the cell containing the query point. It then accesses the next cells closest to the query cell, in a rotating fashion. One rotation covers the cells in the sequence of left, up, right, and down. This process repeats until it finds K (a predefined number) objects. The K objects are then monitored for safe region crossing.

The primary feature of this approach is that the safe region is calculated for the query but not for mobile objects. Thus, in this method, mobile objects do not pay a penalty to monitor safe regions. However, the safe region is larger when compared to the safe region maintained by mobile objects. The larger the safe region, the higher the update message consideration.

Additional query types have also been considered for continuous static query monitoring, including top K queries [37], reverse KNN [50], and detour queries [51]. Each of these approaches tries to reduce the communication cost by reducing the number of update messages received from the mobile objects.

In static query monitoring, the most common approach involves defining a safe region for an object. In most approaches, the safe region is calculated by the server. An MO is responsible for sending an update message whenever that object crosses the boundary of its safe region. This reduces both communication cost and unnecessary update processes.

4.2.2.2 Continuous Monitoring on Moving Queries

Most approaches proposed under the static query do not fit well enough to support this class of queries without modifications (eg, safe region calculation), because of the added mobile feature. This section discusses approaches that address the continuous monitoring on MOs.

Stojanovic *et al.* [52] proposed an algorithm for processing dynamic continuous range queries. This algorithm is based on three steps: the filter step, the prerefinement step, and the refinement step. The filter step and the prerefinement step produce the initial query response. Additionally, these steps check possible overlaps in the query range along each object's path. Detailed information about these overlaps (eg, time and location) is stored in two tables: the continuous range query table and the mobile object table. The refinement step periodically ensures the validity of the entries in these two tables. One primary drawback of this algorithm is the amount of duplicated data managed in memory [52]. As a result, the proposed algorithm is not scalable as the number of objects increases.

Gedik and Liu [53] proposed a distributed approach for RQ to reduce the workload at the server. The server broadcasts the query information upon receiving a new query. Each object then decides whether it is in the query's monitoring region by examining the query information. If the object determines that it is in the monitoring region, then the mobile object keeps that query information. This information will be discarded when the object moves out of the monitoring region. The mobile object estimates the query issuer's position according to the query information received (ie, velocity, time, and position). If this estimated position is different than the one stored, a change in the query result is possible. The object's latest information is passed over to the server. This approach's selective communication with the server reduces the communication cost. However, it violates the query issuer's confidentiality as his or her information is broadcast.

Both SEA-CNN (shared execution algorithm) [54] and SCUBA (scalable cluster-based algorithm) [55] present scalable approaches for continuous query monitoring. SEA-CNN focuses on KNNQ, whereas SCUBA focuses on RQ. SEA-CNN groups queries based on their searching regions and locations. In contrast, SCUBA groups both queries and mobile objects according to their common spatial relationships. As a result, objects and queries could be included in the same group. The performance of each approach is improved when *steady clusters* are present. Steady clusters occur when the set members of a cluster do not change frequently. They are obtained when the object's relative speeds are smaller. When relative speeds are significantly high, objects that were initially in the same group may not remain in the same group. In this case, both the cluster maintenance cost and the query execution cost increase as the number of clusters increases.

Liu and Hua [56] proposed algorithms to process both the dynamic range and KNN queries under road network consideration. The RQ process begins by performing a snapshot query at the server. Objects in the snapshot query result are then notified with the query information (eg, the query position, the query range, and the issuer's speed). Each object updates its information with the server when it moves out of the query range. Upon receiving the update message from an object, the server updates its query result accordingly, and then it updates the object's query list at the server.

KNNQ processing follows a method similar to the RQ. KNNQ is handled as an RQ, where the range is the distance from the query issuer to the furthest vehicle. If a new object can appear in a query result, the current position of each object in the previous result is considered. The new vehicle is then inserted into the appropriate position in the list. This approach performs better when the range is wider as the number of messages to send is lower. However, similar to the approach proposed by Stojanovic et al. [52], this approach maintains a considerable amount of data in memory. This data includes duplicates of object information. For example, each query maintains a list of all of the MOs in the response, and vice versa.

4.2.3 Summary

Most commonly developed continuous monitoring queries include both range and KNN. Some of the approaches for these two are summarized in Table 8. The most common approach for static query monitoring involves defining a safe region for each object. In these approaches, the safe region is generally calculated by the server (which preserves the query issuer's confidentiality). The object is responsible for sending updated messages whenever that object crosses the boundary. This approach reduces communication cost and unnecessary update processes.

In moving query monitoring, some approaches calculate the safe regions at the server. Other approaches broadcast the query information, allowing

Table 8 Continuous Monitoring on Queries Under Fixed Network

Query Algorithm	Query Types	Advantages and Disadvantages
Stojanovic et al.[52]	Range	Distributed approach reduces server work load. Carry significant false positives for individual comparison step privacy violation of query issuer's
Xiong et al. [54]	KNN	Grouping information on spatial relationship gives the scaling up
Nehme and Rundensteiner [55]	Range	Grouping information on spatial relationship gives the scaling up, group maintenance cost is high on dynamic environments
Liu and Hua [56]	Range and KNN	Higher storage cost due to duplicate

the objects to calculate their own safe regions. The broadcast approach both lowers the server-side work load and scales up with the number of mobile objects. This method, however, violates the query issuer's privacy compared to the server-side safe region calculation.

5. QUERY PERFORMANCE OF TRAFFIC PREDICTING QUERIES UNDER ROAD NETWORK CONSTRAINTS

Several of the most relevant queries for road traffic information were selected for simulation purposes. The remainder of this section discusses their performance.

5.1 Snapshot Query Algorithms

Two recent algorithms that provide information about road traffic, ie, query algorithm on R-TPR±-tree [21] and comprehensive algorithm on R^D-tree (also called R^DC-tree) [23] were compared in order to study the effects of individual performance. The experiments were conducted on MO data sets generated by the Brinkhoff's generator [57]. Real road maps of United States were provided to the generator. Data sets were generated by varying three parameters: the number of MOs, the predictive time length, and the road topology. Table 9 shows these parameters and their default values (in bold). The performance was measured in terms of I/O cost, execution time, and query accuracy.

The execution time does not include initial bulk loading of the road map or objects, only the query processing time. The query accuracy was examined by comparing the number of objects in the predictive query results with the actual number of objects on the query road segment at the query time. I/O costs were measured as the number of disk-page accesses performed. Each test case was run for 250 queries and the average cost was reported.

Table 9 Simulation Parameters and Their Values for Snapshot Queries

Parameters	Values
Number of moving objects	10K, 20K, ..., **50K**, 60K, ..., 100K
Predictive time length (in minutes)	10, 20, **30**, 40, 50, 60
Road maps	CO, AR, NM, **CA (California)**

5.1.1 Effect of the Number of MOs

5.1.1.1 Page Accesses

The effect of the number of objects on the average number of page accesses is shown in Fig. 13. The page access count increases slightly with the number of objects. The increase is because these algorithms only access the objects moving on the road segments covered by either the range or the ring, and the portion of increased objects is comparatively smaller. The performance enhancement of the comprehensive algorithm is significant compared to that of the R-TPR±-tree. In fact, the algorithms require about half as many page accesses as the R-TPR±-tree. The reasons are mainly due to the power of the pruning techniques. First, ring queries usually retrieve fewer candidate objects than range queries. Second, arranging the objects according to their traveling directions prevents unnecessary access of objects that are not moving in the same direction. Finally, ordering the objects according to their distance to the destination from the edge helps reduce access of early vehicle destination information.

5.1.1.2 Accuracy

The accuracy of the R-TPR±-tree was considerably far from the correct result (Fig. 14). The traffic reported by the R^DC-tree was very close to the actual traffic on the query road segment. In fact, the accuracy of the R^DC-tree is slightly less than the actual result. The difference is due to the restricted number of hash buckets considered in the R^DC.

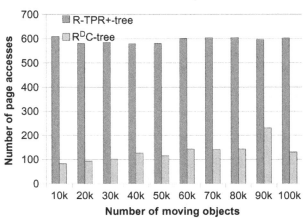

Fig. 13 Effect of the number of moving objects on page accesses.

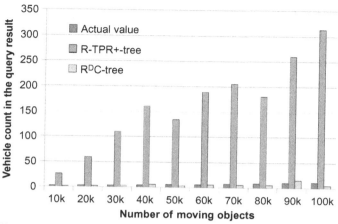

Fig. 14 Effect of the number of moving objects on the accuracy.

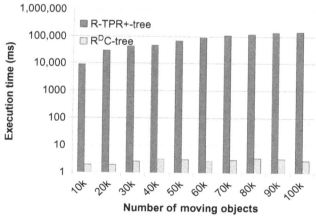

Fig. 15 Effect of the number of moving objects on the execution time.

5.1.1.3 Execution Time

The execution time of each algorithm is presented in Fig. 15; the reported execution time is in logarithmic scale. The figure exhibits the power of the pruning techniques of the proposed algorithms over the R-TPR±-tree.

5.1.2 Effect of the Predictive Time Length

The effect of the predictive time length was studied by varying the length from 10 to 60 min.

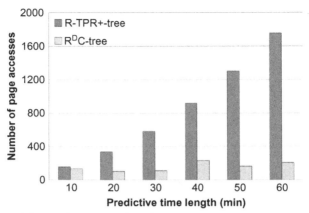

Fig. 16 Effect of the predictive time length on page accesses.

5.1.2.1 Page Accesses

Fig. 16 shows the performance comparison of the R-TPR$\pm$-tree, R^DB-tree, R^DE-tree, and R^DC-tree in terms of the number of page accesses.

Both the R^DC-tree and R-TPR$\pm$-tree access more disk pages when the time length increases. This is because the query range becomes larger when there is more time to look into the future. However, the R-TPR$\pm$-tree's page accesses are increased drastically where the other three algorithms only increase slightly. That is due to the use of ring queries in the R^D-tree query versions. The advantage is more prominent when the length of the query time is longer.

5.1.2.2 Accuracy

Fig. 17 compares the accuracy of the R-TPR$\pm$-tree and R^DC-tree with the actual query result. The results obtained by the R^DC-tree query algorithm are very close to the actual values, and the accuracy is relatively stable for different query time lengths. The minor inaccuracy may be caused by the difference between the estimated traveling routes and the actual routes taken by some objects. The accuracy in the R-TPR$\pm$-tree is much lower than the R^D-tree. The R-TPR$\pm$-tree's query algorithm works well when the predictive time length is extremely short so that the query range mainly covers the road segments next to the queried road segment. The objects in the query range can, at most, move to the next road segment at the query time. When the predictive time length is longer, this estimation introduces many more errors.

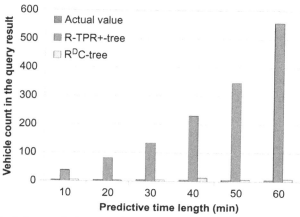

Fig. 17 Effect of the predictive time length on accuracy.

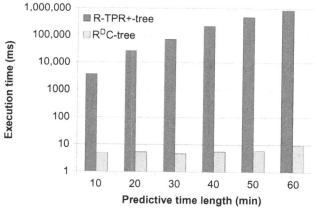

Fig. 18 Effect of the predictive time length on execution time.

5.1.2.3 Execution Time

The execution time for the R-TPR$\pm$-tree increases gradually with the predictive time length. As shown in Fig. 18, the execution times of the other algorithms are relatively steady for all of the predictive time lengths. The performance gap between the two algorithms is enlarged with the increase of the predictive time length.

5.1.3 Effect of the Road Topology

The effect of the road topology was evaluated by testing different road maps: Colorado (CO), Arkansas (AR), New Mexico (NM), and California (CA).

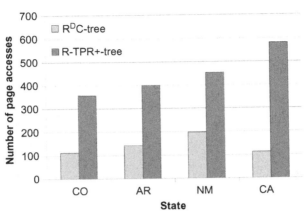

Fig. 19 Effect of the road topology on page accesses.

The average road segment length in these maps varies. They are 0.152 mi. in CO, 0.101 mi. in AR, 0.92 mi. in NM, and 0.81 mi. in CA.

5.1.3.1 Page Accesses

Fig. 19 shows the results for all four topologies. The R^DC-tree significantly outperforms the R-TPR±-tree in all cases. The performances of the R^D-trees are relatively independent of the road topology, while the R-TPR±-tree performs worse when the road segment becomes shorter. This may be because each TPR-tree in the R-TPR±-tree groups the objects better when the road segment is longer. The R^D-tree, on the other hand, results in more objects per hash bucket when the road segment is longer, which negatively affects the performance.

5.1.3.2 Accuracy

As shown in Fig. 20, the query result for the R-TPR±-tree contains a significant number of false positives. The actual value is three-fourths fewer than that of the R-TPR±-tree. However, in terms of execution time, the R^DE-tree is much faster than the R^DB-tree due to the use of the sorting list for pruning vehicles with early destinations. Since the R^DC-tree inherits all of the pruning power of the other two versions, it achieves the overall best performance.

5.1.3.3 Execution Time

As shown in Fig. 21, the execution time of the R-TPR±-tree is in the range of 10–100K ms, while that of R^D-tree ranges 1–10 ms. This significant

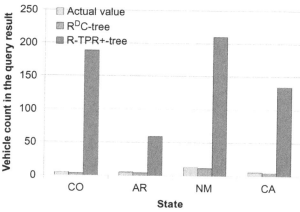

Fig. 20 Effect of the road topology on accuracy.

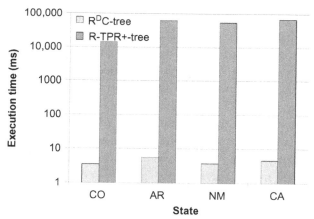

Fig. 21 Effect of the road topology on execution time.

increase in the execution time of the R-$TPR\pm$ is due to the consideration of individual road segment, obtained from the RQ specified by a circle. Since the ring query applied in the $R^D C$-tree reduces the number of edges, the number of individually considered edges is also fewer. Thus, the processing requirements are reduced significantly.

5.2 Continuous Query Algorithms

One of the most recent approaches to providing continuous traffic information (PLQ) [58] on road networks was selected for performance evaluation.

In fact, the most advanced algorithm of the three algorithms proposed in [58], the batch-object (BO) algorithm, was selected and its performance was compared with a naive approach that executes snapshot PLQ [23] after every update message.

This set of experiments was also performed on MO data sets generated by the Brinkhoff generator [57]. The MO data sets were generated using four real road maps selected from different states in the United States. The road maps contain a similar number of road segments but with different topologies. The number of MOs in each data set ranges from 10 to 100K. For each data set, sets of queries were randomly generated by randomly selecting query issuers and queried road segments. The predictive query lengths ranged from 10 to 60 min. Query sets with different number of queries were generated. The chosen parameters and their values are presented in Table 10. The bold values represent the default value for each parameter.

The effects of various factors including the time, the number of queries, the number of MOs, the predictive length, the road topology, and the buffer size are evaluated to measure query performance. Performance was measured in terms of prediction error rate and I/O cost. The error rate was computed by comparing the number of objects in the predictive query results with the actual number of objects on the query road segment at the query time. The I/O cost is the number of disk pages accessed. The reported I/O cost is the average number of pages accessed per query per timestamp. It first calculates the average pages accessed (averaged per query and per timestamp) during each 5-min time interval throughout the query's lifetime ($AvgPg(5 \text{ min})$). The average pages accessed for the entire query lifetime is calculated by taking the average of all 5-min averages in the lifetime of the query.

Table 10 Simulation Parameters and Their Values for Continues Queries

Parameters	Values
Buffer	YES, **NO**
Number of queries	0.5%, 2%, 5%, **20%**, 40%, 60%, 80%, 100%
Number of moving objects	10K, 20K, ..., **50K**, 60K, ..., 100K
Predictive time length	10, 20, **30**, 40, 50, 60 (min)
Road maps	Alpine (CA), Charles (MD), Salem (NJ), **Worth (MO)**

5.2.1 Query Performance over the Query Lifetime

The average prediction error rate and maintenance cost were calculated per timestamp within each 5 min interval for 30 min. The results are reported in Fig. 22.

5.2.1.1 Accuracy

As Fig. 22A shows, the three proposed algorithms consistently yield a much lower prediction error than the naive approach. This is because the naive approach defines the query ring based on the Euclidean distance to the query road segment, whereas the influence regions employed by SU, SO, and BO consider the road distance (which is more accurate) to estimate vehicles that may enter the query road segment. In addition, we can also see that the prediction accuracy of the three algorithms is similar.

5.2.1.2 Page Accesses

Fig. 22B shows the average query maintenance cost. As expected, the proposed three algorithms perform better than the naive approach, and the BO approach performs best. The naive approach needs to execute each query with every timestamp, which may involve duplicate efforts when there is no change in the results. The proposed algorithms utilize the TPR^Q-tree and check all affected queries simultaneously.

For each of these algorithms, including the naive approach, the closer it is to the end of the query's lifetime (ie, the time when the query issuer will enter the querying road segment), the less maintenance cost is needed in general. That is because the influence regions are shrinking as time passes, so the number of objects to be checked decreases. Note that the BO approach shows a slight increase in the maintenance cost at the beginning,

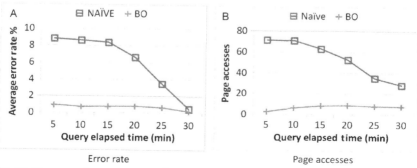

Fig. 22 Query performance over the query lifetime. (A) Error rate. (B) Page accesses.

because the BO approach considers all of the updates issued at one timestamp. The number of updates is fewer when the system first starts because the objects take some time to speed up.

5.2.2 Effect of the Number of Queries

In this round of experiments, we evaluate the effect of the number of queries on the query performance by varying the total number of queries from 0.5% of the total number of MOs to 100%.

5.2.2.1 Accuracy

All four of these algorithms show stable performance in terms of accuracy (s 35(a)). The naive approach, however, yields a higher percentage of error.

5.2.2.2 Page Accesses

As shown in Fig. 23A the naive approach exhibits a relatively stable performance, regardless of the number of queries. This means that the average number of pages accessed per query is independent from the total number of queries being executed. Each query is applied to the same process and

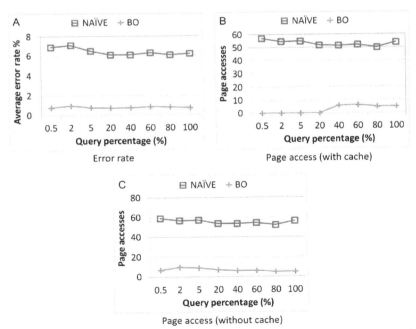

Fig. 23 Effect of number of queries. (A) Error rate. (B) Page accesses (with cache). (C) Page accesses (without cache).

to the same tree (R^D-tree). Hence, the cost depends only on the size of the R^D-tree, but not on the number of queries. However, the proposed SU, SO, and BO approaches access the TPR^Q-tree, and the number of queries stored in the tree changes the tree structure.

5.2.3 Effect of Buffer Utilization

The experiment set conducted in the previous sections was repeated to see the effect of buffer utilization. The employed buffer has a 50 kB capacity and least recently used replacement policy. Fig. 23B reports the query cost for different query percentages with the addition of a buffer.[b] As the figure shows, the query maintenance cost up to 20% is essentially zero, and the rest of the query set shows an increased query cost. The increased costs are comparable to those in Fig. 23C. Comparing Fig. 23B and C, it is clear that use of a buffer improved the query performance up to 20%. This is because, up to 20%, the number of tree nodes in the entire tree structure is less than 50. Thus, the entire tree can be accommodated by the buffer. At most, one disk access is made per one tree node to load the node into the buffer. Once the node is stored in the buffer, no buffer replacement is required. When the number of nodes in the tree exceeds the buffer size, the buffer cannot accommodate all necessary tree nodes simultaneously. Thus, the buffer-miss rate increases, which is why the page access count increases.

5.2.4 Effect of the Number of MOs

In this round of experiments, we evaluate performance when the number of MOs increases from 10 to 100K.

5.2.4.1 Accuracy

Even here, all three algorithms show a competitive accuracy (Fig. 24A). The error rate, in all approaches, increases slightly with the number of objects. This is because the more MOs that are presented, the more uncertainty that exists around the prediction. However, the proposed approaches always achieve a lower error rate for the same reason discussed in the previous section.

5.2.4.2 Page Accesses

Fig. 24B shows the query cost of all four algorithms. According to the graph, one common observation for all algorithms is that they all require a greater

---

[b] Since the accuracy is not affected by the buffer, it is omitted from this discussion.

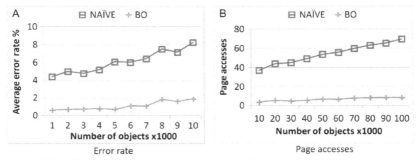

Fig. 24 Effect of number of objects. (A) Error rate. (B) Page accesses.

number of page accesses when the object count is increased. In the naive approach, this happens because the R^D-tree expands the number of objects increases, so the number of node accesses increases. In the proposed algorithms, the TPR^Q-tree structure remains unchanged, but the number of update messages compared to the tree is increased. Another vital observation is that the naive approach gives the worst query cost for fewer objects, and it defeats the performance of SU when the number of objects is increased (approximately at 60K). The reason is that the page access count in the naive approach depends on two factors: the size of the R^D-tree and the number of update messages received. The expansion of the R^D-tree is slower for larger object counts than smaller object counts. This same expansion speed will be applied on the page access count as well. Additionally, the number of update messages is directly proportional to the page access count because the R^D-tree is searched for each update message. However, the SU algorithm also accesses the TPR^Q-tree for each update message. In fact, the SU algorithm accesses the TPR^Q-tree twice for each message. So page access count for the SU algorithm increases at a faster rate than the naive approach. Similarly, the naive approach and SO algorithm performance curves are more likely to be parallel (ie, the same rate). This is because the naive and SO algorithms access their trees once for each message. The gap between the two plots explains the advantage of the TPR^Q-tree over the R^D-tree.

The BO algorithm, on the other hand, behaves entirely different than the other approaches and shows a much better performance. As the figure shows, the BO algorithm was not affected by the number of objects, while the other three algorithms were. In fact, the BO algorithm's performance depends on only the number of different time stamps and it is accountably finite, within the 30-min period. Thus, the BO shows a bounded query cost independent of the number of objects.

5.2.5 Effect of Predictive Time Length

In this set of experiments, the predictive time length is varied from 10 to 60 min.

5.2.5.1 Accuracy

As shown in Fig. 25A the error rate stays in a similar range regardless of the predictive time length in all approaches. This behavior can be explained as follows. For the naive approach, it executes the query for every timestamp, so that any change in the object's travel plan will be captured. Similarly, in proposed approaches, the effect of the object update on the query results at every timestamp is considered.

5.2.5.2 Page Accesses

The predictive time length does affect the query cost as shown in Fig. 25B. The query cost of the naive approach increases when the predictive time length is longer. This is because in the naive approach, a bigger ring query is generated for a longer predictive time length. In the proposed approaches, the query cost also increases with the length of the query window but at a slower rate. This is again due to the advantage of the TPR^Q-tree utilization. The BO's query cost is nearly constant with the predictive time length because it does not depend on the length of the period, but the average number of update messages within the 5-min time interval. Given a fixed number of objects (and assuming the same mobile patterns for any query window size), the average number of messages is independent of the query window.

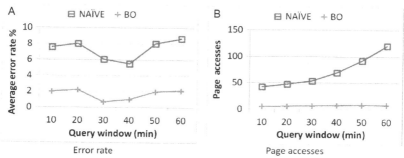

Fig. 25 Effect of predictive time length. (A) Error rate. (B) Page accesses.

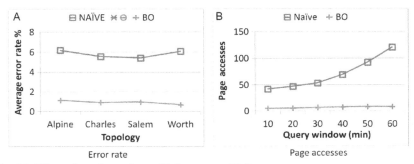

Fig. 26 Effect of road topology. (A) Error rate. (B) Page accesses.

5.2.6 Effect of Road Topology

This section evaluates the effect of the road topology by testing maps for different US counties: Alpine (CA), Charles (MD), Salem (NJ), and Worth (MO). The number of edges in each map was 1576, 1766, 1789, and 1573, respectively, and the average road segment length is 232 m, 370 m, 515 m, and 551 m, respectively.

5.2.6.1 Accuracy

By observing the average rate of error in the individual topologies in Fig. 26A, it can be concluded that the larger the number of edges, the lower the error rate.

5.2.6.2 Page Accesses

Regarding the page accesses as shown in Fig. 26B, BO is relatively independent of the number of edges. However, all three algorithms show better performance when the average road segment length is bigger. This is because, when the road segments are longer, the update messages time interval is spaced out better. Thus, algorithms handle fewer update messages.

6. CONCLUSION AND FUTURE WORK

Traffic-related queries can improve traveler driving experiences. Several research issues need to be addressed to provide a more effective, efficient service to users. One such issue involves constraining the considered mobile environment from Euclidean space to road networks. Another issue includes introducing query types within road-network constraints (eg, traffic-related predictive queries).

This chapter discussed an indexing structure namely an R^D-tree that supports predictive queries on objects moving under road-network constraints. The R^D-tree supports common types of spatial queries (eg, range and KNN) as well as predictive queries (eg, line query). Predictive line queries were addressed under two versions: a snapshot query and a continuous query. Queries embed intelligence by customizing the query result for each user separately. Both the individual's destination and his/her predicted paths are considered for customization. More specifically, a user will obtain only traffic information relevant to his/her route. As a result, the user can adjust the route in favor of either avoiding or moderating the effect of possible traffic.

This chapter also discussed solutions for both of the aforementioned query versions. The snapshot version is addressed with three new algorithms: R^DB-tree, R^DE-tree, and R^DC-tree. They are applied on multiple heuristics whose power is in an increasing order. Due to the most powerful heuristics being applied to the R^DC-tree, it shows the best performance. The approaches for the continuous version were solo update (SU), solo object (SO), and batch object (BO). These three variations were compared together and with a naive approach that repeatedly executes snapshot predictive line queries. Among the three approaches, the BO algorithm reported the best performance, in terms of both page accesses and accuracy.

The scope of this research is open for further exploration and expansion. Some potential areas are listed below:

- The query types addressed in this chapter were user initiated queries. This means the user specifies the road segment that he/she is interested in. When the traffic is estimated for the road segment (for the interested future time), all the current reported object's behavior is assumed to have remained valid. However, some highly dense road segments are possible which might disturb the current assumed moving patterns. This leads to developing methods to identify the mutually independent dense road segment, rather than estimating the traffic of user-defined road segments. Developing efficient techniques to search both time and spatial dimensions would be both an interesting and challenging task.

- The approaches presented in this chapter assumed a centralized server system, which is comprised of a central sever and a group of thin clients. However, with modern technology, most mobile objects are computationally capable for a considerable amount of work. Thus, identifying possible workload distribution for mobile objects would generate promising performance improvement, especially in terms of scalability.

REFERENCES

[1] Research and Innovative Technology Administration (RITA), Bureau of Transportation Statistics, http://www.bts.gov/publications/transportation_statistics_annual_report/2010/pdf/entire.pdf, 2010.

[2] Texas Transportation Institute, Urban Mobility Report, http://www.providenceviaduct.com/resources/2-existing conditions/Urban Mobility Report 2009.pdf, 2009.

[3] Y.N. Silva, X. Xiong, W.G. Aref, The RUM-tree: supporting frequent updates in R-trees using memos, VLDB J. 18 (3) (2009) 719–738. Available at: http://dx.doi.org/10.1007/s00778-008-0120-3.

[4] S. Saltenis, C.S. Jensen, S.T. Leutenegger, M.A. Lopez, Indexing the positions of continuously moving objects, SIGMOD Rec. 29 (2) (2000) 331–342. Available at: http://doi.acm.org/10.1145/335191.335427.

[5] Y. Tao, D. Papadias, J. Sun, The TPR*-tree: an optimized spatio-temporal access method for predictive queries, in: Proceedings of the 29th International Conference on Very Large Data Bases, ser. VLDB'03, VLDB Endowment, vol. 29, 2003, pp. 790–801. Available at: http://dl.acm.org/citation.cfm?id=1315451.

[6] K.S. Bok, H.W. Yoon, D.M. Seo, M.H. Kim, J.S. Yoo, Indexing of continuously moving objects on road networks, IEICE Trans. Inf. Syst. E91-D (2008) 2061–2064.

[7] J. Feng, J. Lu, Y. Zhu, T. Watanabe, Index method for tracking network-constrained moving objects, in: Proceedings of the 12th International Conference on Knowledge-Based Intelligent Information and Engineering Systems, Part II, 2008.

[8] J. Chen, X. Meng, Update-efficient indexing of moving objects in road networks, Geoinformatica 13 (4) (2009) 397–424.

[9] L. Guohui, L. Yanhong, L. Jianjun, L. Shu, Y. Fumin, Continuous reverse K nearest neighbor monitoring on moving objects in road networks, Inf. Syst. 35 (8) (2010) 860–883.

[10] A. Hurson, Y. Jiao, B. Shirazi, Broadcasting a means to disseminate public data in a wireless environment issues and solutions, in: M. Zelkowitz (Ed.), Advances in Computers, vol. 67, Elsevier, 2006, pp. 1–84. Available at: http://www.sciencedirect.com/science/article/pii/S0065245805670015.

[11] J. Zhang, L. Gruenwald, Spatial and temporal aware, trajectory mobility profile based location management for mobile computing, in: Proceedings of the 13th International Workshop on Database and Expert Systems Applications, 2002, pp. 716–720.

[12] S. Chen, B.C. Ooi, K.-L. Tan, M.A. Nascimento, ST2B-tree: a self-tunable spatio-temporal b$^+$-tree index for moving objects, in: Proceedings of the 2008 ACM SIGMOD International Conference on Management of Data, ser. SIGMOD'08. New York, NY, USA, 2008, pp. 29–42. Available at: http://doi.acm.org/10.1145/1376616.1376622.

[13] J.-D. Chen, X.-F. Meng, Indexing future trajectories of moving objects in a constrained network, J. Comput. Sci. Technol. 22 (2007) 245–251.

[14] H. Wang, R. Zimmermann, Processing of continuous location-based range queries on moving objects in road networks, IEEE Trans. Knowl. Data Eng. 23 (7) (2011) 1065–1078.

[15] H. Wang, R. Zimmermann, Snapshot location-based query processing on moving objects in road networks, in: Proceedings of the 16th ACM SIGSPATIAL International Conference on Advances in Geographic Information Systems, ser. GIS'08, 2008.

[16] J.M. Patel, Y. Chen, V.P. Chakka, Stripes: an efficient index for predicted trajectories, in: Proceedings of the 2004 ACM SIGMOD International Conference on Management of Data, ser. SIGMOD '04. New York, NY, USA, 2004, pp. 635–646. Available at: http://doi.acm.org/10.1145/1007568.1007639.

[17] D. Kwon, S. Lee, S. Lee, Indexing the current positions of moving objects using the lazy update R-tree, in: Proceedings of the 3rd International Conference on Mobile Data Management, 2002, pp. 113–120.

[18] C.S. Jensen, D. Lin, B.C. Ooi, Query and update efficient B$^+$-tree based indexing of moving objects, in: Proceedings of the 30th International Conference on Very Large

Data Bases, ser. VLDB'04, VLDB Endowment, vol. 30, 2004, pp. 768–779. Available at: http://dl.acm.org/citation.cfm?id=1316689.1316756.

[19] M.L. Yiu, Y. Tao, N. Mamoulis, The Bdual-tree: indexing moving objects by space filling curves in the dual space, VLDB J. 17 (3) (2008) 379–400.

[20] Y. Tao, D. Papadias, X. Lian, Reverse KNN search in arbitrary dimensionality, in: VLDB, 2004, pp. 744–755.

[21] J. Feng, J. Lu, Y. Zhu, N. Mukai, T. Watanabe, Indexing of moving objects on road network using composite structure, in: Knowledge-Based Intelligent Information and Engineering Systems, 2007, pp. 1097–1104.

[22] D. Papadias, Qiongmao Shen, Yufei Tao, K. Mouratidis, Group nearest neighbor queries, in: Proceedings of the 20th International Conference on Data Engineering, 2004, pp. 301–312. 30 March–2 April.

[23] L. Heendaliya, D. Lin, A. Hurson, Predictive line queries for traffic forecasting, in: Transactions on Large-Scale Data and Knowledge-Centered Systems, 2012.

[24] D. Papadopoulos, G. Kollios, D. Gunopulos, V. Tsotras, Indexing mobile objects on the plane, in: Proceedings of 13th International Workshop on Database and Expert Systems Applications, 2002, pp. 693–697.

[25] S. Saltenis, C.S. Jensen, Indexing of moving objects for location-based services, in: Proceedings of the 18th International Conference on Data Engineering, ser. ICDE'02, 2002, pp. 463–472.

[26] A. Guttman, R-trees: a dynamic index structure for spatial searching, in: SIGMOD'84, Proceedings of Annual Meeting, Boston, Massachusetts, June 18–21, 1984.

[27] H. Samet, The quadtree and related hierarchical data structures, ACM Comput. Surv. 16 (2) (1984) 187–260.

[28] Y. Xia, S. Prabhakar, Q+Rtree: efficient indexing for moving object databases, in: Proceedings of the Eighth International Conference on Database Systems for Advanced Applications, 2003.

[29] C. Jensen, D. Lin, B.C. Ooi, R. Zhang, Effective density queries on continuously moving objects, in: Proceedings of the 22nd International Conference on Data Engineering, ICDE'06, 2006.

[30] R.A. Finkel, J.L. Bentley, Quad trees: a data structure for retrieval on composite keys, Acta Inform. 4 (1) (1974) 1–9.

[31] S. Chen, C.S. Jensen, D. Lin, A benchmark for evaluating moving object indexes, in: Proceedings of the VLDB Endowment, 2008.

[32] K.-S. Kim, S.-W. Kim, T.-W. Kim, K.-J. Li, Fast indexing and updating method for moving objects on road networks, in: Proceedings of the Fourth International Conference on Web Information Systems Engineering Workshops, 2003.

[33] J. Chen, X. Meng, Y. Guo, S. Grumbach, H. Sun, Modeling and predicting future trajectories of moving objects in a constrained network, in: Proceedings of the 7th International Conference on Mobile Data Management, ser. MDM'06, 2006.

[34] D. Pfoser, C.S. Jensen, Indexing of network constrained moving objects, in: Proceedings of the 11th ACM International Symposium on Advances in Geographic Information Systems, 2003.

[35] E. Frentzos, Indexing objects moving on fixed networks, in: T. Hadzilacos, Y. Manolopoulos, J. Roddick, Y. Theodoridis (Eds.), Advances in Spatial and Temporal Databases, ser. Lecture Notes in Computer Science, Springer, Berlin/Heidelberg, 2003.

[36] V.T. De Almeida, R.H. Güting, Indexing the trajectories of moving objects in networks, Geoinformatica 9 (2005) 33–60.

[37] K. Mouratidis, M.L. Yiu, D. Papadias, N. Mamoulis, Continuous nearest neighbor monitoring in road networks, in: Proceedings of the 32nd International Conference on Very Large Data Bases, ser. VLDB'06, 2006.

[38] P. Fan, G. Li, L. Yuan, Y. Li, Vague continuous K-nearest neighbor queries over moving objects with uncertain velocity in road networks, Inf. Syst. 37 (2012) 13–32.

[39] N. Beckmann, H.-P. Kriegel, R. Schneider, B. Seeger, The R*-tree: an efficient and robust access method for points and rectangles, in: Proceedings of the 1990 ACM SIGMOD International Conference on Management of Data, 1990.

[40] J. Le, L. Liu, Y. Guo, M. Ying, Supported high-update method on road network, in: 4th International Conference on Wireless Communications, Networking and Mobile Computing, WiCOM'08, 2008.

[41] H. Kejia, L. Liangxu, Efficiently indexing moving objects on road network, in: International Conference on Computational Intelligence and Software Engineering, CiSE, 2009.

[42] D. Stojanovic, A.N. Papadopoulos, B. Predic, S. Djordjevic-Kajan, A. Nanopoulos, Continuous range monitoring of mobile objects in road networks, Data Knowl. Eng. 64 (2008) 77–100.

[43] H. Jeung, M.L. Yiu, X. Zhou, C.S. Jensen, Path prediction and predictive range querying in road network databases, VLDB J. 19 (2010) 585–602.

[44] J. Dai, C.-T. Lu, Dime: disposable index for moving objects, in: Mobile Data Management (MDM), 2011 12th IEEE International Conference on, 2011.

[45] S. Prabhakar, Y. Xia, D.V. Kalashnikov, W.G. Aref, S.E. Hambrusch, Query indexing and velocity constrained indexing: scalable techniques for continuous queries on moving objects, IEEE Trans. Comput. 51 (10) (2002) 1124–1140.

[46] Y. Cai, K.A. Hua, An adaptive query management technique for real-time monitoring of spatial regions in mobile database systems, in: Proceedings of 21st IEEE International Performance, Computing, and Communications Conference, 2002.

[47] Y. Cai, K. Hua, G. Cao, Processing range-monitoring queries on heterogeneous mobile objects, in: Proceedings of the 2004 IEEE International Conference on Mobile Data Management, 2004.

[48] H. Hu, J. Xu, D.L. Lee, A generic framework for monitoring continuous spatial queries over moving objects, in: Proceedings of the 2005 ACM SIGMOD International Conference on Management of Data, ser. SIGMOD'05, 2005.

[49] K. Mouratidis, D. Papadias, M. Hadjieleftheriou, Conceptual partitioning: an efficient method for continuous nearest neighbor monitoring, in: Proceedings of the 2005 ACM SIGMOD International Conference on Management of Data, ser. SIGMOD'05, 2005.

[50] T. Xia, D. Zhang, Continuous reverse nearest neighbor monitoring, in: Proceedings of the 22nd International Conference on Data Engineering, ICDE'06, 2006.

[51] S. Nutanong, E. Tanin, J. Shao, R. Zhang, R. Kotagiri, Continuous detour queries in spatial networks, in: IEEE Transactions on Knowledge and Data Engineering, 2012.

[52] B.P.A.N.P.D. Stojanovic, S. Djordjevic-Kajan, A. Nanopoulos, Continuous range query processing for network constrained mobile objects, in: 8th International Conference on Enterprise Information Systems (ICEIS), 2006.

[53] B. Gedik, L. Liu, MobiEyes: a distributed location monitoring service using moving location queries, in: IEEE Transactions on Mobile Computing, 2006.

[54] X. Xiong, M.F. Mokbel, W.G. Aref, Sea-cnn: scalable processing of continuous k-nearest neighbor queries in spatio-temporal databases, in: Proceedings of the 21st International Conference on Data Engineering, ser. ICDE'05, 2005.

[55] R. Nehme, E. Rundensteiner, SCUBA: scalable cluster-based algorithm for evaluating continuous spatio-temporal queries on moving objects, in: Y. Ioannidis, M.H. Scholl, J.W. Schmidt, F. Matthes, M. Hatzopoulos, K. Boehm, A. Kemper, T. Grust, C. Boehm (Eds.), Advances in Database Technology—EDBT 2006, Springer, Berlin, Heidelberg, 2006.

[56] F. Liu, K.A. Hua, Moving query monitoring in spatial network environments, Mob. Netw. Appl. 17 (2) (2012) 234–254.

[57] T. Brinkhoff, A framework for generating network-based moving objects, 2004. Available at: http://www.fh-oow.de/institute/iapg/personen/brinkhoff/generator.

[58] L. Heendaliya, D. Lin, A. Hurson, Continuous predictive line queries for on-the-go traffic estimation, in: Transactions on Large-Scale Data and Knowledge-Centered Systems, 2014.

[59] L. Qin, J.X. Yu, B. Ding, Y. Ishikawa, Monitoring aggregate K-NN objects in road networks, in: Proceedings of the 20th International Conference on Scientific and Statistical Database Management, ser. SSDBM'08, 2008.

ABOUT THE AUTHORS

Lasanthi Heendaliya received her PhD in Computer Science from Missouri University of Science and Technology in 2015. Her primary research interests are in Mobile databases, Big Data, Distributed Computing, and Parallel Computing. She received her MS in Computer Science from St. Cloud State University in 2009 and her BE in Computer Engineering from the University of Peradeniya, Sri Lanka in 2006. She is currently working as an adjunct teaching professor at the University of Missouri–St. Louis.

Michael Wisely received BS degrees in Computer Science and Computer Engineering from the Missouri University of Science and Technology in 2012. He is currently a PhD candidate in Computer Science at Missouri S&T, where he is a GAANN Fellow and a Chancellor's Fellow. His research interests include traffic modeling and distributed computing. He is a member of IEEE and ACM.

Dan Lin is an associate professor and Director of Cybersecurity Lab at Missouri University of Science and Technology. She received the PhD degree in Computer Science from the National University of Singapore in 2007, and was a postdoctoral research associate at Purdue University for 2 years. Her main research interests cover many areas in the fields of database systems and information security.

Dr. Sahra Sedigh Sarvestani is an Associate Professor of Electrical and Computer Engineering and a Research Investigator with the Intelligent Systems Center at the Missouri University of Science and Technology. Her current research centers on development and modeling of dependable networks and systems, with focus on critical infrastructure. She received the BS degree from the Sharif University of Technology and the MS and PhD degrees from Purdue University, all in electrical engineering. She is a Fellow of the National Academy of Engineering's Frontiers of Engineering Education Program and held a Purdue Research Foundation Fellowship from 1996 to 2000. She is a member of HKN and ACM and a senior member of the IEEE.

A.R. Hurson is a professor of departments of Computer Science, and Electrical and Computer Engineering at Missouri S&T. For the period of 2008–2012 he served as the computer science department chair. Before joining Missouri S&T, he was a professor of Computer Science and Engineering department at The Pennsylvania State University. His research for the past 33 years has been supported by NSF, DARPA, Department of Education, Department of Transportation, Air Force, Office of Naval Research, NCR Corp., General Electric, IBM, Lockheed Martin, Penn State University, and Missouri S&T. He has published over 320 technical papers in areas including database systems, multidatabases, global information sharing processing, cyber-physical systems, application of mobile agent technology, object-oriented databases, Mobile and pervasive computing, computer architecture and cache memory, parallel and distributed processing, dataflow architectures, and VLSI algorithms.

AUTHOR INDEX

Note: Page numbers followed by "*t*" indicate tables.

SUBJECT INDEX

Note: Page numbers followed by "*f*" indicate figures, and "*t*" indicate tables.

CONTENTS OF VOLUMES IN THIS SERIES

Volume 71

Programming Nanotechnology: Learning from Nature
    BOONSERM KAEWKAMNERDPONG, PETER J. BENTLEY, AND NAVNEET BHALLA
Nanobiotechnology: An Engineers Foray into Biology
    YI ZHAO AND XIN ZHANG
Toward Nanometer-Scale Sensing Systems: Natural and Artificial Noses as Models for
Ultra-Small, Ultra-Dense Sensing Systems
    BRIGITTE M. ROLFE
Simulation of Nanoscale Electronic Systems
    UMBERTO RAVAIOLI
Identifying Nanotechnology in Society
    CHARLES TAHAN
The Convergence of Nanotechnology, Policy, and Ethics
    ERIK FISHER

Volume 72

DARPAs HPCS Program: History, Models, Tools, Languages
    JACK DONGARRA, ROBERT GRAYBILL, WILLIAM HARROD, ROBERT LUCAS,
    EWING LUSK, PIOTR LUSZCZEK, JANICE MCMAHON, ALLAN SNAVELY, JEFFERY VETTER,
    KATHERINE YELICK, SADAF ALAM, ROY CAMPBELL, LAURA CARRINGTON, TZU-YI CHEN,
    OMID KHALILI, JEREMY MEREDITH, AND MUSTAFA TIKIR
Productivity in High-Performance Computing
    THOMAS STERLING AND CHIRAG DEKATE
Performance Prediction and Ranking of Supercomputers
    TZU-YI CHEN, OMID KHALILI, ROY L. CAMPBELL, JR., LAURA CARRINGTON,
    MUSTAFA M. TIKIR, AND ALLAN SNAVELY
Sampled Processor Simulation: A Survey
    LIEVEN EECKHOUT
Distributed Sparse Matrices for Very High Level Languages
    JOHN R. GILBERT, STEVE REINHARDT, AND VIRAL B. SHAH
Bibliographic Snapshots of High-Performance/High-Productivity Computing
    MYRON GINSBERG

Volume 73

History of Computers, Electronic Commerce, and Agile Methods
    DAVID F. RICO, HASAN H. SAYANI, AND RALPH F. FIELD
Testing with Software Designs
    ALIREZA MAHDIAN AND ANNELIESE A. ANDREWS
Balancing Transparency, Efficiency, and Security in Pervasive Systems
    MARK WENSTROM, ELOISA BENTIVEGNA, AND ALI R. HURSON
Computing with RFID: Drivers, Technology and Implications
    GEORGE ROUSSOS
Medical Robotics and Computer-Integrated Interventional Medicine
    RUSSELL H. TAYLOR AND PETER KAZANZIDES

Volume 94

Volume 95

Volume 96

Volume 97

Volume 101

Printed in the United States
By Bookmasters